MIRACLE MUTTS

Laura Greaves is a multi-award-winning journalist, author and proud 'crazy dog lady'. She has spent nearly twenty years writing for newspapers and magazines in Australia and around the world and is the former editor of *Dogs Life* magazine. Now a freelance writer, Laura has written extensively for countless dog and pet-specific print and web publications. She is the author of the collections *Incredible Dog Journeys*, *Dogs with Jobs* and *The Rescuers*, the children's book *Amazing Dogs with Amazing Jobs*, as well as three romantic comedy novels, *Be My Baby*, *The Ex-Factor* and *Two Weeks 'Til Christmas*, all of which feature an extensive supporting cast of cheeky canines.

Also by Laura Greaves

Incredible Dog Journeys
Dogs with Jobs
The Rescuers
Amazing Dogs with Amazing Jobs

MIRACLE MUTTS

LAURA GREAVES

MICHAEL JOSEPH
an imprint of
PENGUIN BOOKS

MICHAEL JOSEPH

UK I USA I Canada I Ireland I Australia
India I New Zealand I South Africa I China

Michael Joseph is part of the Penguin Random House group of companies,
whose addresses can be found at global.penguinrandomhouse.com.

Penguin
Random House
Australia

First published by Michael Joseph, 2019

Text copyright © Laura Greaves, 2019

The moral right of the author has been asserted.

Cover design by James Rendall © Penguin Random House Australia Pty Ltd
Cover photograph courtesy dezy/Shutterstock
Typeset in Sabon and Brandon Grotesque by Midland Typesetters, Australia
Printed and bound in Australia by Griffin Press, an accredited ISO AS/NZS 14001
Environmental Management Systems printer.

A catalogue record for this
book is available from the
National Library of Australia

ISBN: 978 0 14379 316 8

penguin.com.au

MIX
Paper from
responsible sources
FSC® C009448

Underdog: *(noun)* A competitor thought to have little chance of winning a fight or contest.

Miracle: *(noun)* A remarkable event or development that brings very welcome consequences.

*When you're an underdog,
you're forced to try things you would
never otherwise have attempted.*
— Malcolm Gladwell

CONTENTS

INTRODUCTION

Stories of miraculous dogs are everywhere, if you know where to look for them. Sometimes they're big, headline making, truly awe-inspiring – like the tales that make up this book.

But other times they're small and quiet. They might just be sweet examples of a canine's triumph over illness or injury, or a routine set of circumstances that lead to a nice outcome for a four-legged friend. At first glance these stories might not look especially miraculous at all.

But they are.

How do I know this? Because I've been lucky enough to meet a handful of four-legged miracles in my life. I recognise them as miracles because, without some small element of chance, my life – and theirs – would have been very different indeed.

My first doggy miracle was Robbie the West Highland white terrier. I got him for Christmas when I was ten, and we loved each other with a ferocity unique to kids and their first dog.

Tragically, just a year later, Robbie was run over and died. The driver who hit him did not stop, and my devastation was mixed with a cold fury at the injustice of it all. I was so angry that I wrote an impassioned letter to my local newspaper condemning that driver. It was published, and the paper's editor called me to tell me how deeply my letter had touched her. It was the very first time my name appeared in print, and my first inkling of the power of the written word. It sparked in me a burning desire to tell stories that would move people.

Would you be reading this book if I hadn't loved and lost Robbie? There's no doubt in my mind that the loss of my first dog set me on the path to where I am today, writing books about dogs that have changed lives. In that sense, while Robbie's death was heartbreaking, it was also miraculous.

Today I'm fortunate to have three miracles walking around my house. A Nova Scotia duck tolling retriever, Tex is twelve years old, and there is no earthly reason why he should still be here. He has arthritis, hypothyroidism, an anxiety disorder, leukaemia, an incurable lung disease and epilepsy. As I was writing this book he inexplicably developed blood poisoning and almost lost his life yet again. His vets are permanently baffled as to how he just keeps on keeping on. He is a medical marvel; my fluffy, cantankerous miracle boy.

His younger sister, Delilah, also a toller, has had her share of miraculous near misses, too. She once leapt on a

revolting rotten apple core in the gutter and inhaled it –
literally – before I could stop her. It lodged in her windpipe
and she choked. A frantic dash to the vet and $3000
emergency surgery are the only reason she's still with me.

My latest miracle mutt bounced into my life on 4 March
2019 – the very day I began writing this book. It was a
Monday, and still oppressively hot where I live in the
Blue Mountains, just west of Sydney, even though it was
technically autumn at last.

I had taken Tex and Delilah to the local vet for their
routine vaccinations. Thanks to my illness-and-injury-
prone pair, the staff at the vet know me well. It's got to
the point where I can ring up and say, 'Hi, it's Laura' and
they immediately know who I am and which dogs I'm
calling about.

On this afternoon I was sitting in the consulting room
with Delilah while Tex was out the back having his shots
when I heard a sudden commotion out in the reception area.

The consulting room door was open a crack, and through
it I could see that a woman had arrived at the clinic carrying
a red plastic cat carrier and an enormous cardboard box.

The lady explained to the practice manager that she had
found four kittens on the side of the road in the blazing
afternoon sun. They were without water or shelter, and
there was no sign of their mothers.

That's right, *mothers* – plural. These babies had been
dumped together, but they weren't from the same litter. One
was a ginger boy who looked to be four or five weeks
old. He was lively and alert and meowing most indignantly.

The other three were much younger; their eyes were open, but only just. They were grey tabbies, and almost unbearably cute.

The woman had rescued them from the roadside, but she couldn't keep them as she had dogs at home. She was en route to the local council animal shelter with them when it occurred to her to call ahead and check that they would accept the forlorn felines.

The shelter was happy to take them, the good Samaritan reported, but they closed for the day at 3.30 p.m. That was just ten minutes from now – and the shelter was a thirty-minute drive away. She wouldn't make it in time.

'Could the babies stay at the clinic overnight instead?' she asked.

I'm sure you can imagine that by this point I was a mess of warm fuzzy feelings. What a kind thing this woman had done! She had saved four lives! My bubble was promptly popped a moment later. The vet brought Tex back to me, then went out into the reception area to talk with the lady. Gently, he explained that there was unfortunately little the clinic could do for the tiny cats.

The ginger boy seemed reasonably healthy, but the three really young ones were so small and weak they would need two-hourly bottle-feeding overnight. Who knew how long they'd been out there in the heat before the woman had picked them up?

There would be nobody at the clinic from 7 p.m. until 7 a.m. the next day, and staff weren't able to take the little creatures home because of the risk of exposing their own pets to disease. Left alone overnight, the outlook for the kittens was bleak.

And even if all four cats somehow made it through the night, nobody was able to leave the clinic to make the hour-long round trip to the shelter with them the next day.

I knew what was coming next, but my heart still sank when I heard the vet say that humane euthanasia might be the kindest option for the kittens. At least then they would drift peacefully off to sleep instead of dying of exposure, dehydration or worse.

It's a very human thing to root for the underdog – or undercat, in this case. Five minutes earlier I hadn't even clapped eyes on these kittens, but in that moment I felt I would have done almost anything to save them.

It's worth mentioning here that I am extremely allergic to cats. If I'm coming to your house and you have a cat, don't bother putting him outside during my visit. Don't even bother vaccuming. If a cat has so much as *looked* at your home in the last five years, I'll be a wheezing, sneezing, watery-eyed mess within two minutes of walking in the front door.

My five-year-old daughter is also very allergic to cats. Plus we have the aforementioned two dogs, whose innate retrieverness compels them to chase cats whenever possible.

I was *not* the right person to have four kittens requiring round-the-clock hand-feeding in my home. So what did I do? If you think I burst into the reception area and pleaded with the vet to let me have four kittens requiring round-the-clock feeding in my home, you're absolutely right.

I'd like to think the vet was moved by my passion (though it's possible he was in fact slightly frightened by my fervour). Either way, we reached a compromise. While he was adamant he couldn't let me take the kittens home because of the disease risk, he promised he'd do everything he could for them before the clinic closed for the night. I would then come back the next morning and drive them to the shelter.

I took my dogs home and tried not to think about the kittens all night. (I thoroughly failed at this.)

The next morning I returned to the clinic – and got the bad news. Sadly, the three smallest kittens hadn't made it. Their condition had deteriorated rapidly in the evening and there was no option but to put them to sleep. This wasn't unexpected, but my heart still sank.

The good news, however, was that the little ginger ninja was doing well. He was bouncy and curious and in fine voice as I strapped his carrier into my passenger seat and set off for the shelter.

This is where the story really begins! (Oh, did you think this was a tale about cats? Silly! This is a *dog* book!)

I arrived at the shelter less than half an hour after it opened for the day. I took my little orange friend in his carrier up to the reception desk.

And then I fell in love.

The local council's animal control officer was also waiting at the desk. He was clutching a leash, and at the end of that leash was a young female kelpie mix. She was jet black with the most soulful brown eyes I had ever seen.

I don't know what to tell you. Something *happened* to me in that moment. I've truly never felt an instant connection with a dog the way I did that day.

Of course, the dog didn't care one iota. She was too busy leaping around like a kangaroo and licking everything in sight. She was *perfect*.

I asked the animal control guy what her story was. He told me that he'd just picked her up from a vet clinic about 30 kilometres away. She'd been seen roaming around that area for three or four days before someone was finally able to catch her and take her to the clinic.

She wasn't microchipped. She was wearing a collar, but didn't have an ID tag. I was positive somebody was missing her. She was too adorable and appeared too well cared for to have been dumped. Her people would find her, I was sure of it.

And so I gave her a scratch behind the ears as she was whisked off to the kennel, then wished my feline friend a long and happy life and went on my way.

That probably should have been the end of the story. But it wasn't.

Days later, I could not stop thinking about the dog. I called the shelter to find out if she had been reunited with her owners, and was surprised when the shelter manager said there had been no enquiries about her.

I live close to where the dog was found roaming and had been keeping an eye out for the lost dog posters I was sure would soon appear. They didn't. Nor were there any frantic posts about a missing kelpie cross in any of the local pet groups I follow on social media.

I asked the shelter manager what would happen next, and she said the dog would remain under a 'stray hold' for another week. If she wasn't claimed within that time, she would become the property of the shelter and they would assess her suitability for adoption.

I called back in a week. Of *course* I did!

Still nobody had come for her. She now belonged to the shelter. They had named her Audrey.

Casually, I asked when she would be available for adoption. That's when the manager dropped a bombshell: Audrey had managed to scale the eight-foot fences of her enclosure and flee more than once. Thankfully she was quickly grabbed and brought back each time, but clearly she was suffering pretty severe anxiety.

'I'm sorry to tell you,' she said, 'that the outlook for her is not positive.'

This was now a problem for me. I already had two dogs, both seniors, one very sick. Plus I had a husband and a child and two guinea pigs and a goldfish and a book to write.

I. Did. Not. Need. To. Rescue. A. Dog.

But everything was telling me I was supposed to rescue this dog. If I didn't do something, Audrey would be lumped in the too-hard basket and her life would literally be over.

I had to do it. I just had to.

I'm possibly the least assertive person in the world. I am always accommodating, unfailingly polite, and avoid confrontation at all costs.

Unless there's a dog involved.

For weeks, I made a complete pest of myself. I called, I emailed, I wrote actual letters. I lobbied to be allowed to visit Audrey even though they don't usually let people visit dogs that aren't adoptable.

The funny thing is, I was imagining that the shelter staff thought I was utterly painful. I figured they must resent my constant contact, my wheedling, my badgering. But I was mistaken. They loved it! They were thrilled that I was pushing so hard to save her, grateful for my agitation. They didn't want to see Audrey put down any more than I did, but they were bound by their own policies.

In the end, they had to lodge a special request with their executive management to have Audrey ruled adoptable in spite of her escape artistry and anxiety. A month after I met her, the higher-ups finally gave the green light. It truly felt like a miracle.

Audrey – whose name is now Coco – came home with me on 8 April 2019. She is heaven – just the sweetest, cuddliest dog ever. Delilah absolutely adores her. Even Tex is grudgingly fond of his young sidekick. In fact, I think he's actually become livelier and more playful since Coco arrived.

So that's the story of Coco, my third miracle dog. On the face of it she didn't do anything spectacular, unless you think that escaping death is spectacular – which I do. Coco was an underdog in every sense, but she not only survived, she is thriving. So many strange, tiny things had to happen in such a precise, magical order for Coco to have the life she has now. Her story will never grace the front page of a newspaper or go viral online, but she is here, and that is miraculous. The universe is a marvel.

Look at your dog right now and know what a miracle it is that you found each other. Know that your tail-wagging pal thinks you are magic. As you read this collection of stories about dogs like Coco – dogs that weren't supposed to make it, dogs that had to conquer enormous odds – I hope you'll remember that often all it takes to make a miracle is one person who cares. A person like you.

Laura Greaves
2019

PS The ginger kitten was adopted by his foster family and he's doing great!

MAGGIE

From being shot on the streets of Beirut to working as a therapy dog in the UK

It's not that people were cruel to dogs where Kasey Carlin grew up in the United States. The majority of dog owners dutifully covered the essentials, providing food and shelter, rudimentary though it may have been. Many even took their canine companions for a walk every now and then.

But while most people didn't hurt their dogs, from Kasey's perspective it didn't feel like they really *loved* them either. Not enough to let them indoors during winter to curl up on the sofa. Not enough to take them to the vet when they were sick; ailing or old dogs were more likely to be taken to a shelter or abandoned in rural areas than treated.

In the part of Indiana where she spent her formative years, Kasey observed dogs being treated more like property than part of the family. 'I grew up with dogs chained up in the backyard and people dumping their animals. That was the culture,' she says.

It was upsetting for someone who had always felt an almost spiritual connection to the feathered, furred and finned. Her affinity with animals even led her to study animal behaviour at university.

'I've always been with animals. I've had dogs and cats. I've kept chickens in the bathroom. I'm quite happy to catch animals that need help,' says Kasey. 'My dad used to tell me, "Even if you see Bambi on the road, leave it!" but I don't care if I get bitten.'

So when she followed her mum to the United Kingdom at the age of fifteen, Kasey experienced culture shock in the best possible way. 'When I moved to the UK I was amazed to see how much everyone here adores their animals compared to where I come from.'

Kasey and her mum settled in Brighton, a seaside resort town on England's south coast, some 75 kilometres from London. Kasey worked as a dog groomer and later started her own outdoor doggy daycare business, spending her days getting out and about with a pack of enthusiastic pups.

With her growing business and busy lifestyle, Kasey was content not to have a dog of her own – she certainly wasn't starved for canine company after all. But as often happens when we open our hearts to dogs, the universe had other plans.

She fostered her first dog when a prospective daycare client reached out to Kasey saying she was in dire need of help with her anxious dog.

'This lady messaged me saying her dog was very fearful. It had been rescued from overseas, where it was kept in a crate, and she couldn't do anything with it,' she recalls. 'I've always taken on the problem dogs, whether they're fearful or dog aggressive.'

The woman had adopted her dog from the Wild at Heart Foundation (WAHF), a London-based charity that funds and supports animal welfare projects all over the world. The charity was founded by celebrity florist Nikki Tibbles, best known for her opulent flower shop, Wild at Heart, in London's Notting Hill. WAHF's mission is to reduce the world's 600-million-strong stray dog population through rescue projects, desexing programs, awareness campaigns and education initiatives.

Kasey met the dog in question and could see the owner had the best intentions, but she was overwhelmed by the extent of her pet's trauma and unable to provide the type of specialist care needed. So Kasey agreed to foster the anxious pooch until WAHF could find a forever family that had more experience with special needs dogs.

That first dog opened the fostering floodgates. Kasey continued to foster dogs through WAHF. She really liked the charity's commitment not just to saving dogs in other countries, but also working to empower people in those countries to better care for animals within their own communities.

'I've worked with a lot of charities, and a lot of them take these dogs out of the country, but they're not actually fixing the problem there,' she explains. 'They're saving one dog's life, which is great, but if every undesexed dog has had six puppies, in six years that's 45 000 dogs.'

(WAHF, meanwhile, is part of the 'Spayathon for Puerto Rico' initiative, which aims to desex 20 000 animals in under-served communities across Puerto Rico.)

In 2018, Kasey took in Mishka, an Alaskan Klee Kai who arrived with some fairly significant behavioural issues.

Kasey wanted to give Mishka the time and attention she needed to become a confident and well-adjusted pet, plus she already had two other elderly dogs at home, one of which, Ted, was nearly blind. So she reluctantly told WAHF she couldn't foster any more dogs for at least a year.

But once again, the universe had other ideas.

Just four months after Kasey took in Mishka, her mum saw a post on the WAHF website about a dog in desperate need.

The female dog was in a shelter in Beirut, the capital city of Lebanon. She had been found chained to a box, with one ear missing and rampant infections in both eyes that had left her blind. Though she had been treated with antibiotics, the dog's eyes were all but obliterated. She was also pregnant.

The dog was thought to be between three and five years old. 'Three with a hard life, five if she'd been a pet at some point,' says Kasey.

Cruel treatment of both wild and domestic animals is a serious problem in Lebanon. The trade of rare animals including lions and tigers is big business, but even animals traditionally kept as household pets are often not well cared for or outright abused. There is also an enormous stray dog and cat population across the country.

Lebanon only enacted its first animal protection laws in 2017, but in the same year sickening video footage of stray dogs being poisoned by municipal staff sparked outrage around the world.

There are few animal shelters in a country still rebuilding after decades of civil conflict, and those that do exist are under resourced and overwhelmed. Dogs that escape cruelty or death on the unforgiving streets are certainly not assured of safety in a shelter.

A WAHF volunteer who visited shelters in Lebanon told Kasey there wasn't a single dog in the facility that was 'whole' – all of the animals were missing eyes, ears or limbs.

Unsurprisingly, the blind, pregnant dog was not doing well in the chaotic shelter environment. Staff had posted her picture on a local pet rescue website in an effort to find her a quiet, calm foster home in which she could hopefully recover. They had named her Angie.

In London, animal lover Roxana Ghiassee was relaxing in the bath when the harrowing pictures of Angie appeared on her phone. Roxana had recently adopted her own dog from Beirut, Cookie, and remained deeply concerned about the plight of stray dogs in Lebanon.

'She was in the bathtub reading this awful story about sad little Angie, and I don't know why but she was just compelled to help her,' says Kasey. 'I'm so glad she did.'

Roxana had some connections in Beirut and she used them to have Angie moved from the shelter to a foster home *cum* private boarding facility. Then she got to work contacting rescue groups and charities in the UK.

It proved to be a frustrating exercise, at least at first. 'Roxana messaged so many charities asking for help, but nobody would help because on paper Angie was not adoptable,' Kasey explains. 'Nobody wants the old, blind, abused dog – but Roxana was very determined not to let Angie stay out there.'

The pictures of her injuries suggested Angie would need surgery, but was she strong enough to survive it? And even if she did pull through, she was unlikely to find a home in Lebanon with owners willing to give her the patience and understanding she would need in order to overcome her terrible past. Convinced the UK was Angie's only hope, Roxana kept pushing.

Finally, she found WAHF, which promptly agreed to help bring both Angie and another blind street dog, Romeo, to the UK. But first they had to raise the money for their medical care and the transport needed to get the pair out of Beirut.

A crowdfunding campaign raised nearly £5000 to cover the costs. It then took six months to navigate the necessary bureaucracy and ensure both dogs had all the required paperwork and vaccinations for entry to England.

While she waited for her flight to freedom, Angie underwent surgery to properly clean and close her eyes. Not only were her open wounds unsightly, they left her vulnerable to recurrent infection. Sadly, her unborn puppies had to be euthanised in order for Angie to receive the life-saving surgery.

'Her eyes had rotted away so there was nothing there, but the lids had just been left open. While she was in the public shelter Roxana had been saying, "Are you serious? Nobody is going to adopt her looking like that,"' says Kasey.

During that operation, veterinarians made a horrifying discovery: Angie had four bullets lodged in her eye sockets.

She had been shot repeatedly and left for dead.

'She had been living with those bullets in her eyes for months, and nobody knew. She never bit anyone and she never made a sound,' Kasey says. 'She probably understood that if she made a noise she became prey. That's why it can be so hard for vets to diagnose animals. I can't even imagine the agony Angie was in.'

The bullets were extracted and what was left of Angie's right ear was removed and the wound cleaned up. Vets confirmed the loss of the ear was no accident: it had been intentionally cut off. They also discovered her jaw had been fractured at some point; it had healed badly and many of her teeth were broken. They suspected she had either been beaten or hit by a car.

Kasey finds it hard to even imagine the kind of human who would inflict such cruelty on a chained, defenceless animal.

'Did they take her somewhere, shoot her and dump her, or was she just shot on the street? You just think, *Why would they do that?*' she says. 'That's not going to kill a dog – it's just pure torture.'

Her growing legion of fans waited with bated breath on the day of Angie's surgery. She had survived so much horror already, but in her weakened, traumatised and terrified state there was no guarantee Angie would survive it.

But Beirut street dogs are nothing if not tough. Against the odds, Angie made it through. As long as she remained in Lebanon she was at risk every day, but Roxana at last had some hope that Angie might get the happy ending she deserved.

That was when the call went out to WAHF supporters for a foster home in the UK – and Kasey's mum saw the post.

'When she'd had her surgery they booked her flights, then posted and said, "Can anybody help?" but nobody offered to foster her. Mum sent me her pictures and I didn't look at them all day, because I knew that would be it,' says Kasey with a laugh.

'Mum was always the one saying, "Do you really need to foster another dog?" so for her to want to foster, I knew we'd end up doing it. She does adore animals, but she's not got the experience to foster an old, blind dog. In the end I said, "Okay, I'll do it."'

Now came the hardest part: waiting.

As she loitered in the car park of a petrol station near London's Heathrow Airport, Kasey thought about what a strange situation she had found herself in.

Not long ago she had known next to nothing about the plight of street dogs in Lebanon. Now she was something of an expert, and she was waiting to meet a flight from Beirut that carried a dog she'd never met but had already fallen in love with.

Despite offering Angie a home, she realised she really knew nothing about her. 'All I'd read was that she'd been shot and she was very afraid. In the entire time that she stayed with the lady out in Lebanon she never left the house because she was too afraid,' Kasey says.

It was 18 September 2018, and Kasey remembers it like it was yesterday. 'I was so excited that I was two hours early and I sat in the van just waiting for that text,' she says.

Roxana had travelled from London to Beirut to bring back Angie and check on Romeo, who had been beaten, shot in one eye and confined to a tiny bathroom for most of his life. (He made it to the UK in November, where he was adopted by an adoring London family and renamed Solo.)

She had promised to text Kasey as soon as the flight touched down. It would be the first time Kasey would meet Angie's saviour in person after months of communication.

Kasey tried to imagine what life would be like with a blind, abused dog. 'From what I'd read I thought all she'd want would be a nice couch to sit on, good food, and a bit of love,' she says. 'I thought if I could get her to a point where she could take a walk around the block and be happy with that, then that would be a nice life for her.'

After what seemed an eternity, Kasey's phone trilled with the news that Angie was officially on British soil. She raced to the Heathrow Animal Reception Centre, which processes all animals entering the UK.

More waiting followed while Angie's paperwork was checked, and then finally the door swung open and out she came.

It was an incredibly emotional moment.

'Because she's blind she would kick her feet really high in front of her when she walked, I guess to see if anything is there,' says Kasey. 'So she came out kicking her legs, and Roxana just ran to her, bawling her eyes out.'

Roxana wasn't the only one in tears. 'There wasn't a dry eye in the place. We'd told the airport staff Angie's story and everyone was just crying over this little dog,' she says.

That's right: *little* dog. Angie's remaining ear looked so enormous in photos that Kasey had thought she was a large breed dog, similar in size to a German Shepherd or a Labrador. (Her precise breed mix is unknown beyond the generic 'Beirut street dog'.)

In fact, Angie was tiny.

'I was so shocked at how small she was. She'd been on this plane and through all this upheaval, and she was so little. She had no idea who I was, and she barely knew Roxana – she had only met her that day,' says Kasey. 'I went to say hello to her and it was just instant love.'

For her part, Angie clearly didn't want to waste any time. Though she couldn't see Kasey, she immediately cuddled up to her. 'Anytime she meets anybody she just sticks her head into them. She'll try to burrow into people,' she says.

Finally, it was time to go home. Kasey has a large van for her daycare business and expected to put Angie securely in the back of it for the ninety-minute drive back to Brighton.

But Angie wasn't keen on that idea. 'Roxana had put her in the front seat footwell in Lebanon, so I put blankets down and she just sat there. I just talked to her the whole drive,' she says. 'I just wanted her to know that I was there for her and that I was going to give her a good life. She'd met a lot of not-nice people and I'm sure she's a very good judge of character. I just wanted to comfort her.'

Her mum was waiting at home, excited to meet the new addition to the family whose safe arrival in Britain she had played such a key part in. Mother and daughter had done their research about introducing a blind dog to a new environment.

'Because we'd had Ted we kind of knew the issues visually impaired dogs have, but we had never had a dog that was completely blind,' says Kasey. 'We were advised to keep Angie in one room at a time and let her map out her environment. We decided the kitchen would be her first room so that she could go straight out the back door to use the bathroom.'

The first time Angie stepped into the Carlins' grassy backyard to answer the call of nature must have been a revelation.

'Roxana later told me that Angie had never seen a park or anything close to it, so it was probably the first time she had touched proper grass instead of just a few weeds. She must have felt like, *What is this? What have you put me on?*'

As their first order of business, Kasey decided to change Angie's name. She had a friend called Angie and it seemed strange to have a dog with the same name. Besides, Angie had overcome enormous odds to leave her awful former life behind for a fresh start in the UK. It was only fair she mark her metamorphosis with a new name.

'Mum and I had come up with all these names and she ignored all of them, but when I said "Maggie" she looked up,' Kasey says. 'I'm pretty sure it's only because it sounds like Angie, but I said, "That's it! That's your name!"'

If Kasey had imagined that Maggie would be disoriented or agitated on her first night in her new home, she needn't have worried. The brave little dog was exhausted from her long journey to safety, and the bombardment of new sounds and smells.

'I put Maggie in her crate and I remember she just did a very quiet little whine, then went to sleep and slept all night,' she says. 'I can't imagine what was going through her head, but she was just so accepting.'

Maggie may have been accepting, but resident dog Mishka certainly was not – at least not at first. Kasey's only real concern when offering to foster Maggie was how her first baby would cope with her new canine sibling. Mishka went everywhere with Kasey, including to work every day, and with her history of behavioural issues there was no guarantee she would tolerate another dog on her turf.

Kasey decided not to introduce the dogs on Maggie's first night in the house, preferring to wait until they could meet on neutral territory. Even then, their early interactions didn't inspire confidence.

'They hated each other!' Kasey laughs. 'It was a month before they got used to each other, and it took them a long time to understand each other.'

The animosity wasn't just coming from Mishka. Maggie would often growl at her four-legged housemate, which Kasey thinks was probably a defence mechanism given she can't see and therefore couldn't read Mishka's body language.

Maggie was also not a fan of Mishka's chatter. Husky breeds are known for being vocal and Mishka certainly likes to 'talk', but Maggie didn't know what to make of it at first and interpreted it as a threat.

'Mishka talks all the time, so it was a matter of getting Maggie used to that. She was like, *Oh wow, you're growling at me – I'll fight you!*' she says. 'She's lovely, but she's tough. She's been a street dog and she's been in a pound. She would have been scrapping all the time in Beirut.'

As her dogs struggled to find common ground, Kasey tried to be practical. It didn't really matter if Maggie and Mishka never became friends, she reasoned. Maggie was a foster dog, after all – her stay in Brighton was never supposed to be permanent.

But for all her rational thinking, Kasey was disappointed – because she wanted Maggie to stay forever.

'I had it in my head that she was my foster dog and I was going to do everything I could to help her go on to the next stage. I wanted her, but I knew it wasn't necessarily the best thing for her or for Mishka,' she says. 'If she didn't fit in with the family that was okay, but we *would* find her a family and in the meantime she'd have a home with us.'

And then one day, something shifted. Kasey had taken both Mishka and Maggie to work with her, and the seating arrangements in the van had been a source of stress. Mishka had always ridden shotgun – perched on the front passenger seat – but since Maggie's arrival she had been relegated to the footwell while Maggie claimed the seat. Kasey would usually separate them when she left the van to collect a daycare client.

'One day I was rushed so I went in to pick up a dog and thought, *Okay, I'll try leaving them together*. It's a confined space, so it was the ultimate test,' she says. 'When I came back they were both on the front seat and Mishka had her head on Maggie. I thought, *Okay, they're friends*.'

Life at home became more harmonious, too. 'I never thought I would be able to feed them in the same room, and then all of a sudden they were eating treats next to each other,' says Kasey.

'Now they just love each other. They're really symbiotic. While Mishka helps Maggie, Maggie does just as much for Mishka because she's so friendly. She's brought her out of her shell with people.'

As Maggie and Mishka's friendship blossomed, Kasey felt hope blossoming too. She had drafted many an email to WAHF during Maggie's first few weeks in Brighton asking to formally adopt her, but with the dogs' relationship so fractious she hadn't allowed herself to press send.

But now she wondered if perhaps she and her mum could be Maggie's forever family after all.

Finally, on 17 October, she took the plunge. 'Multiple

times a day I'd write these messages and never send them. Eventually I said, "Take her off the website – she's mine!"' she says.

Kasey was adamant she would pay Maggie's full adoption fee. She felt it was the least she could do after so many kind strangers had donated their hard-earned money to save Maggie from an unthinkable fate in Lebanon.

And then it was official: Maggie was a member of the Carlin clan. The hostile streets of Beirut were 4500 kilometres and a lifetime away.

In many ways it felt like Maggie had always been part of the family, but there were frequent reminders that her life had not always been so full of love.

When she first came to live with Kasey, Maggie would have nightmares. Her little legs would pump furiously as if running and she would whine in distress. Kasey wonders if she was reliving the panic of being chased by the people who hurt her in Beirut.

But the night terrors paled in comparison to the shocking discovery Kasey made shortly after Maggie's arrival from Lebanon.

'She's got scars all over her face, and I noticed a strange tuft of fur on her right side and flicked it over to see if there was another scar there,' she says.

But it wasn't a scar that caused Maggie's fur to stand on end. It was a small, hard lump under her skin, like a ball bearing – or a bullet.

Kasey ran her hands all over Maggie's body to see if she could feel any more lumps. With each new swelling her fingertips grazed, the ghastly truth hit home.

Maggie was riddled with bullets. She has thirteen bullets still lodged in her flesh, as well as the four taken out in Lebanon.

'I started feeling them and I just thought, *Oh god, she's got more bullets in her.* Most of them are behind the ear that's missing and in her neck, plus a few on the left side of her shoulder and in her chest,' says Kasey. 'She has a very prominent one on her right side above her ribs.'

The good news is most of the bullets can be removed, and will be when Maggie has further surgery to repair her smashed teeth. In the meantime, they don't cause her any pain or disrupt her day-to-day life.

Kasey was stunned when she found the bullets, and not just because of the abhorrent cruelty that had put them there. What was even more remarkable than her ability to soldier on after being shot seventeen times was the fact that she did it happily. Everything Maggie does, says Kasey, she does with an attitude of gratitude and love.

'Ever since I adopted her she's just got more and more courageous. When people see her in the street they don't realise she's blind,' she says. 'I take her to the park in the morning and she will walk straight into a crowd of people to get love. She's just like, *You will love me – and you have no choice in the matter!*'

Sometimes people are taken aback when they notice that Maggie is heavily scarred, short one ear and doesn't have eyes, but Kasey says their shock never seems to register with her beloved pooch.

'She doesn't know what she looks like – she's just beautiful. She has these perfect imperfections.'

Maggie's gentle nature and unquenchable joie de vivre have even led her to become a therapy dog. Kasey's mum works in a care facility and Kasey frequently takes Maggie to visit its residents.

'She will walk those halls without a lead because she knows exactly where she's going. She knows every room that's got one of her friends in it, and she will lead the way. She walks in and goes, *Right, where's my love?* She adores people,' she says.

Maggie also visits nearby Sussex University at exam time to offer moral support and stress-busting cuddles to students.

Kasey never worries about Maggie when they're out and about, despite her disability. Maggie is extremely intelligent and Kasey has worked hard to give her the skills she needs to find her way in the world. She knows the commands *left, right, step up, step down* and *stop* (which is employed often to prevent Maggie from bumping into things).

As often happens when one of the five senses is removed, Maggie's other senses have heightened and she navigates via smell, sound and even touch. She doesn't do her quirky high-kicking walk anymore, nor does she growl at unfamiliar dogs. Maggie is confident about the world around her, and her place within it.

'Everywhere we go, she goes off lead. She will follow me in a crowd even if I don't call her or make any noise.

She'll be in a pack of dogs and will lead the pack even if we're somewhere we've never been before,' says Kasey. 'When we go out in the countryside she'll walk where the grass has been tamped down by other walkers, then if she goes over into the taller grass she'll correct herself.'

It's no longer just Kasey's friends and family and people in the Brighton area who can share in Maggie's incredible transformation from abused street dog to adored therapy pet. Soon after her arrival in the UK, Kasey started an Instagram account for Maggie (@maggiethewunderdog). She was reluctant to start with, because in the back of her mind was the possibility Maggie wouldn't be staying for good, but she wanted to document the little dog's extra-ordinary progress.

Her account biography says, 'The heavier the rain, the brighter the rainbow.' It's a perfect summary of Maggie's life. The account now has more than 180 000 followers, and Kasey regularly receives beautiful messages from people all over the world whose hearts have been touched by Maggie's message of courage and resilience.

'I only agreed to foster Maggie because I thought nobody else would. Nobody wants a Maggie; they all want poodles and French bulldogs. To rescue a blind, abused dog – nobody wants that,' she says.

'Instagram has become this little place where we can show people that it doesn't matter if your dog's not pedigree. So many people have messaged me and said they wake up every morning and check Instagram just for Maggie. The kindness of people is just so amazing.'

The miracle of Maggie is not just that she survived being shot, mutilated and blinded. It's not just that she made it out of Lebanon, a country with notoriously few protections for animals. It's not even just that a Beirut street dog is now a UK therapy dog, or that she has become a social media star.

All of these things *are* objectively miraculous. Maggie could have lost her life at any time in myriad equally terrible ways. But she is still here, bringing joy to everyone lucky enough to meet her.

No, the real miracle of Maggie is this: none of it matters to her. The cruelty she endured, the pain, the fear and uncertainty – it is irrelevant to Maggie. It is very relevant to *us*, of course: humans absolutely must ensure the unconscionable treatment of vulnerable creatures like Maggie does not continue.

But Maggie couldn't care less. She is here. Now. And she is loved.

'Everything I ever thought Maggie would be, I was wrong. I have honestly never met a dog like Maggie. She's the piece we didn't know was missing,' says Kasey. 'She doesn't judge. Dogs don't care who you are – they just want to know if you're going to love them.'

Nor does Maggie bear a grudge. Above all else, her tale is about forgiveness.

'I honestly feel that if Maggie met the person who did this to her, she'd be as forgiving towards them as she is to anyone else,' she says. 'Maggie has chosen to forgive people, so I think she should share that message of forgiveness.'

Is there any greater miracle than that?

CHARLIE PUCCINI

From being run over by three trains to fighting fit

The message came through at 10.56 p.m. on a stormy Wednesday in late summer.

'*Oh, Laura,*' it said. '*Our beloved Charlie escaped during the storm – nearly two years to the day after his escape in the* last *storm! We can't believe it. We're so upset and waiting with fingers crossed.*'

The missive came from Ann Paynter, who I was due to interview the following morning. I had arranged to chat with Ann about her dog, Charlie Puccini, who had made headlines in 2017 with a truly remarkable survival story. Charlie's return to Ann and children Jake, Sophia and Lucy after that escapade had been nothing short of miraculous.

And now he had vanished again, lost in the bush at the foot of the vast NSW Blue Mountains almost exactly two years after his first ordeal. What were the chances?

My heart sank. Though I hated to admit it, I didn't like Charlie's odds of finding his way home this time. Could one little dog expect to receive a second miracle?

All any of us could do was wait to find out.

Summer is undoubtedly dazzling all over Australia, but as anyone who's ever spent the season in Sydney will attest, it's particularly spectacular in the harbour city.

It's not just the beaches, though they are definitely breathtaking. It's not the footpaths crowded with al fresco diners, or the long balmy evenings, or the barbeque dinners in the park either (but they're all pretty great, too).

No, there's one thing that Sydney does, if not better, then certainly on a grander scale than most Australian cities in summer: thunderstorms.

Sydney's fierce storms are a sight – and sound – to behold. Dense black clouds roll in, usually in the late afternoon, bringing with them sheeting rain and hailstones the size of golf balls. The wind roars as the stifling humidity gives way to window-shaking thunder and a light show that would give the famous New Year's Eve fireworks a run for their money.

And then, just as quickly as it advanced, the storm charges out to sea. All is once again still. A Sydney storm is like a holiday romance: intense, maybe even a little bit frightening, but brief.

The afternoon of 22 March 2017 delivered a typically ferocious tempest, and the St George-Sutherland region south of the city was right in its path. The area is the fifth most storm-affected in the state, and the suburb of Yarrawarrah – where Charlie Puccini lived at the time – is smack bang in the middle.

Ann Paynter was on her way home from work when the sky unleashed its fury that Wednesday. She was immediately worried, because spaniel–terrier mix Charlie is petrified of thunderstorms – and he was home alone.

'No one was home; we were all at work and school. It was a terrible storm. I remember being at Strathfield train station, about 30 kilometres from Yarrawarrah, and thinking, *Oh, that's a cracker,*' she says.

Ann had watched Charlie desperately try to claw his way into a wardrobe to hide during previous storms, so she knew he'd be feeling terrified. She just hoped that, if he'd been left in the backyard that morning, one of the kids would be home soon to bring him into the sanctuary of the house.

Charlie had always been quite a character. He came with the name Charlie Puccini – Yvonne, Ann's friend and Charlie's former owner, gave him the Mediterranean-inspired moniker because he loves Italian food – but Charlie *Houdini* might have been more fitting given his penchant for unscheduled adventures.

One of Yvonne's beloved dogs had recently passed away when a work colleague found Charlie roaming the streets of Kings Park in western Sydney in April 2013. Her colleague suggested Yvonne offer the forlorn stray a home, and she readily agreed.

Nobody knew for sure how long Charlie had been wandering, where he'd escaped from, how old he was – they guessed around two years old – or even his precise mix of breeds.

'We definitely think he has some fox terrier in him, because he's a real hunter – he loves to hunt lizards and things,' says Ann. 'We thought perhaps he might be part Cavalier King Charles Spaniel as well. He's got these massive furry feet.'

Charlie stayed with Yvonne for a while, but although she loved him dearly her other resident dogs did not. Around the same time, Ann's youngest daughter, thirteen-year-old Lucy, was dropping some heavy hints about getting a dog.

'Lucy's dad and I had always had dogs, but we hadn't had one for a couple of years and Lucy was saying, "I really want a puppy,"' she says. 'I happened to be out to dinner with Yvonne not long afterwards and she said, "I have to find a new home for Charlie." He just wasn't getting on with her other big dogs.'

So it was decided that Charlie would move in with the Paynters – on one condition. 'When he came to us Yvonne said, "You must keep the name." She has a wicked sense of humour,' says Ann.

She agreed and Charlie moved in. For a while all was calm. The children doted on Charlie Puccini – and they weren't the only ones. Ann's son, Jake, and his girlfriend, Pierra Bell, regularly took the little dog to visit people in aged care homes.

'He's the kind of dog that just melts people's hearts,' Ann says.

Though Charlie clearly knew he had it made with his new family, apparently old habits died hard: he couldn't ignore his innate desire to explore the world beyond the Paynter household, and managed to abscond a handful of times. How he managed it was something of a puzzle, because the backyard was securely fenced. But however he was able to flee, the important thing was he always came back.

Until the day of the storm.

As Ann had hoped when the storm broke, it wasn't long before one of the kids arrived home – but there was no sign of Charlie.

'I was on my way home on the train when Sophia rang and said, "Charlie's gone." Our garden fencing was solid, but he got out somehow,' she says. 'He had a habit of running around and coming back again, so at first nobody was too worried.'

But as the minutes ticked by with no sign of Charlie, everybody became very worried indeed. The storm had long passed, but he hadn't returned.

Ann's mind raced with possibilities. What if the torrential rain had washed away his scent and he couldn't retrace his steps? What if he'd been injured in the inclement weather? Charlie was registered and microchipped, but what if someone had picked him up and spirited him away?

By 7.30 p.m., panic had well and truly set in. And then the telephone rang. It was the vet at Engadine Veterinary Hospital, just a kilometre away.

'We've got your dog, Charlie,' he told Ann.

They were the words she had been hoping to hear, but something in his tone made her cautious. Ann's heart was in her throat as she asked, 'Is he okay?'

'No,' came the grave reply.

There was a long pause.

'He's been hit by a train.'

Sydney's Illawarra train line has been ferrying passengers from Central station in the heart of the CBD to Waterfall, the last suburb officially classified as part of the Sydney metropolitan area, since 1884.

Today known as the T4, it is the second busiest line in the Sydney Trains network, with travellers racking up more than 69 735 000 trips per year. It's also consistently one of the city's most reliable lines – packed commuter trains thunder along the tracks at up to 130 kilometres per hour every few minutes during peak times.

It is really not, then, an ideal place for a scared and disoriented 7-kilogram dog to set up camp in the middle of a raging thunderstorm.

Unfortunately Charlie Puccini didn't get that memo.

His family didn't know it at the time, but when Charlie dug or climbed or battered his way out of the Paynters' backyard and disappeared into the storm, he ran about 5 kilometres towards the train line.

Ann has no idea why he went that way – and she doesn't think it was a conscious decision on Charlie's part either.

'He would have just been so hyped up on adrenaline,' she says.

Yarrawarrah doesn't have its own train station; it is equidistant from both Loftus and Engadine stations. The rail corridor between those two stations is bordered on one side by the teeming Princes Highway and on the other by the 150-square-kilometre Royal National Park.

Roaring traffic or dense bush – it's unlikely that either option would have seemed appealing to the terrified Charlie. Add the driving rain and howling wind, and the fact that storm had reduced visibility and cast everything in an eerie glow, and it was nothing short of a horror movie for a little dog.

Perhaps that's why, when he found himself on the railway tracks, Charlie decided to stay put. It would have been comparatively quiet there, and it was open country – Charlie could see quite a way in either direction. It must have felt like the safest option while he figured out what to do next.

That could explain Charlie's actions in the minutes that followed.

When a bright light appeared in the distance, Charlie didn't move. As the light drew nearer and the steel tracks on either side of him began to thrum, he was still. When the speeding juggernaut attached to the now blinding light sounded its horn, Charlie gave no ground.

Even as the train bore down on him and Charlie locked eyes with its frantic driver, he stayed exactly where he was.

Was he frozen with fear? Did he somehow think he was a match for than 330 tonnes of locomotive? Ann says

Charlie was used to cars stopping to let him cross the road at the local park; perhaps in his confused state he imagined the train would do the same.

Whatever was racing through his doggy brain in that moment, Charlie stayed resolutely on the tracks, staring the train down as it hurtled towards him.

The train struck him, knocking Charlie flat onto the sleepers between the rails.

The horrified train driver was fully aware he had just run over a dog. He knew the dog must be dead – it was inconceivable to him that such a tiny creature could survive that catastrophic impact. And though he knew the collision was unavoidable, he couldn't help but replay the awful moment in his mind. The way the dog had looked at him was eerie. *Why didn't it move*, he thought. *Why didn't the horn scare it off the tracks?*

Devastated, the driver radioed ahead to Engadine station to report what had happened. Even if nothing could be done for the dog, hopefully its owners could be informed of its sad fate.

The awful news was relayed to a Sydney Trains incident commander called Simon. He moved quickly, in part because a dead animal on the tracks was a hazard, but also because he was hoping for a miracle.

Access to busy metropolitan train tracks is understandably restricted, so it wasn't easy for Simon to reach the dog.

'He got in his ute and raced up to the location the driver had given, then he had to walk through the bush,' says Ann.

When he reached the spot, Simon saw crows circling overhead. He knew they were hoping to make a meal of the crumpled figure on the tracks.

But the birds would have to wait, and so would he, because there was another train approaching. Simon could hardly bear to watch as the behemoth rumbled over the dog. Even if by some incredible stroke of luck the dog was still alive, there was surely no way it could withstand a second strike and live.

When the train had passed, Simon risked a glance. From his vantage point, he thought the first train driver was correct in his assessment: the poor dog had not survived the initial hit. The second train seemed to have rolled over without contact, but the dog was unnervingly still.

Simon grabbed a towel from his vehicle and headed for the rail line. But then a shrill whistle stopped him in his tracks.

To his dismay, a *third* train was advancing. It too passed over the dog at speed, taking with it Simon's last shred of hope for the dog's wellbeing.

When at last the line was clear, he moved towards the dog. He was almost afraid of what he would find when he got close.

And then – was that movement?

Yes!

Incredibly, Simon saw a flicker of life. The dog's eyes were open and bulging, and his leg appeared to be badly damaged. As gently as he could, Simon wrapped the stricken canine – which he could now see was male – in the towel. He placed him in his ute and raced to the closest vet hospital.

Ann's phone rang a few minutes later.

Ann couldn't make sense of what she was hearing.

Charlie was at Engadine Veterinary Hospital. He'd been run over. By a car, surely?

'By a train,' the vet repeated.

Ann burst into tears. How on earth had Charlie managed to get himself run over by a *train*? She could barely bring herself to ask the question, but she had to know.

'Is he dead?'

'No, he's not,' came the reply. 'But he's not responding. I'm sorry, but you should prepare for the worst.'

Ann gathered the kids and together they made the terrible journey to say what they thought were their final goodbyes. Hospital staff worked feverishly to save Charlie, but they didn't expect him to make it through the night.

If he *did* manage to hang on until morning but still showed no signs of recovery, the vet advised that putting Charlie to sleep might be the kindest option. The Paynters agreed to talk it over and let him know their decision the next day.

In the meantime, Ann got in touch with Simon to find out more. She had been shocked to learn that Charlie had been struck by one train, but was utterly astonished when Simon told her a total of three trains had run over her precious dog.

Ann marvelled at Charlie's luck – both the series of unfortunate events that took him to the tracks in the first place, and the incredibly *good* luck that saved his life.

'From what we could tell, the first train knocked him flat and the others went straight over him. If he'd been a bigger dog, like a Labrador, he would have been killed,' she says.

The following morning, the family returned to the hospital. It seemed so unfair that he had survived his ordeal only to face a slow demise in a clinic, and so Ann and the kids had made the painful decision to let their brave boy go if his condition hadn't improved.

When they arrived, Charlie was indeed still gravely ill. The vet told the Paynters there was nothing more that could be done.

Heartsick, they took the unconscious Charlie out of his cage for one last cuddle. Young Lucy was inconsolable – Charlie belonged to the whole family, but he was *her* dog really; the one she had wanted so badly.

'Lucy and Pierra sat with him. They put him on Lucy's lap and she was crying and saying, "Charlie, Charlie,"' says Ann.

It was a touching, if tragic, moment. But nobody – not even the vet – could believe what happened next.

'Charlie just opened his eyes and started licking her arm. It was amazing, totally miraculous,' she says. 'I was just astounded. I thought, *Wow, Charlie is really meant to be here.*'

Three fully laden passenger trains were evidently no match for Charlie Puccini. Even after he regained consciousness, however, the vet urged caution. Charlie was awake, but he was by no means out of the woods.

'Even though he was still alive, the vet said he could still go because of trauma to the brain. They just had to wait and see – it was a case of time will tell,' says Ann. The children kept vigil by his side, and by Saturday Charlie was eating again.

'We thought he was going to be severely brain damaged, but he just isn't. By day three he was staggering around. He kept walking sideways, but apart from that he was the same old Charlie.'

After four days in hospital, Charlie came home. He had escaped minus one toe, probably lost when he put his paw up in an instinctive effort to halt the first train. But that first collision was likely a glancing blow rather than a full impact. It's a miracle he survived the former; he certainly would not have lived through the latter.

Within a couple of months, it was as if the nightmare had never happened. As well as concerned friends and family, there was one person in particular Ann made sure to keep updated on Charlie's progress.

'The poor train driver had been just devastated. He said he had seen the look in Charlie's eyes right before the train hit him,' she says. 'We certainly let him know that Charlie recovered.'

'He was found this morning, three suburbs away!'

It had been a long twelve hours, much of which I'd spent rolling my eyes at myself for losing sleep over a stranger's missing dog (#crazydoglady). But Charlie had been through so much already; it just seemed entirely unfair that he might yet be denied the long, happy life he deserved.

So when my phone trilled with Ann's message at 10.26 a.m. on Thursday morning, I was genuinely overjoyed.

When we spoke, Ann sounded thrilled – if a little exasperated with her adventurous dog.

This time, mercifully, there had been no trains involved. But Charlie had managed to scarper from Ann's new home at Leonay, in Sydney's western suburbs at the bottom of the Blue Mountains, crossing a freeway and heading straight up through the bush to the village of Blaxland.

Ann admits she thought Charlie's luck had finally run out.

'My partner had got home from work and within the space of half an hour Charlie got out. It got darker and darker. Lucy was crying,' she says. 'We thought, *Not again – this is it, he won't come back to us this time.*'

Several families in Ann's street headed out into the gathering darkness to search for Charlie by torchlight. Meanwhile, Ann posted appeals on a local lost pets page on Facebook and called every vet in the area.

Finally, at 11.30 p.m., Charlie himself reached out for help. 'He had run 11 kilometres and was at the back door of a lovely young girl's house at Blaxland, barking to be let in,' she says. 'She said he was covered in burrs, twigs and thistles.'

Ironically, the good Samaritan who took Charlie in for the night immediately shared his picture to Facebook – but she posted on a page for Blue Mountains pet owners, while Ann had posted to a western suburbs group.

His temporary guardian took him to her local vet first thing; it was the only vet in the area Ann hadn't called.

Fortunately, Ann had updated Charlie's microchip with her new address. 'The vet rang at ten and said, "I think I've got your dog,"' she says. 'When he came home he just slept all day. He knew he was in trouble.'

He may have his moments, but Charlie Puccini is a treasured member of the family. 'He's very protective of his backyard and of all of us,' says Ann. 'He is super sweet and so cute.'

But with two miraculous returns from disaster under his belt, this prodigal pooch has lost some privileges when it comes to stormy weather.

'We've decided he must always be put inside even if it looks like the slightest chance of rain,' she laughs.

Seems like a small price to pay for a lifetime of love.

FERGUS

From abused stray to therapy dog for burns survivors

In Australia, the golden retriever is one of the top ten most popular breeds for people looking for a family pet (it's number six on the list, to be precise). There are more than 200 registered breeders across the country, many of whom have long waiting lists of prospective owners eager to pay $3000-plus for a puppy. Unsurprisingly, it's not often that these handsome dogs are surrendered to shelters or picked up as strays.

In other parts of the world, however, it can be a very different story. In Turkey, for example, there are hundreds of golden retrievers living on the streets and in shelters. Many are sent to the United States for rehoming – one Istanbul rescue alone has sent more than 1000 dogs to the US since 2015.

'Goldies' are the third most popular dog breed in the US, but even there they can find themselves without a permanent place to call home. Often, they have been bought as adorable fuzzy puppies, then discarded by owners unable or unwilling to cope with their adult size and energy levels.

In one three-year study of a Pennsylvania animal shelter, golden retrievers made up 7.5 per cent of the canine residents. They were that shelter's third most-surrendered breed; only Labrador retrievers and German Shepherds fared worse.

Of course, it's not all bad news. Millions of golden retrievers are loved beyond measure and doted on by their families every day of their lives. And for those that aren't so lucky, well, there are plenty of people in their collective corner.

The Golden Retriever Club of America has its own rescue committee. Its job is to support nearly 100 individual breed rescue groups working across the nation to find new homes for abandoned or abused goldies. One of those groups is Southern California Golden Retriever Rescue (SCGRR), based in Los Angeles.

And on 15 August 2015, SCGRR happened to be in the right place at the right time to help a young goldie in desperate need.

Like many major cities the world over, the sprawling City of Angels is divided up into local government areas called counties. Each county has its own animal control department, and most operate at least one shelter that takes in stray and surrendered dogs, cats and other animals.

Los Angeles County is the most populous county in LA (and in fact in the entire US), with more than 10 million inhabitants. It has seven shelters, and in the 2018–19 financial year they took in 36 818 animals. Five thousand of those were dogs surrendered by their owners, while another 11 000 were strays. More than 14 000 dogs were returned to their owners or adopted to new families, but nearly 2000 were euthanised.

On that steamy August day, volunteer Barry Jacobs had driven two hours to LA County's Lancaster shelter on behalf of SCGRR to pull a golden retriever. (Independent rescue groups frequently pull animals from county shelters, placing them in foster homes while they work to get them adopted.)

While he was there, a dog in the facility's holding area caught Barry's eye. Stray animals awaiting claim by their owners are housed in this area for a legally mandated period of time. If an animal is not claimed, staff then decide whether it is suitable for adoption or should be humanely euthanised, usually for medical or behavioural reasons.

Barry *thought* this dog was a purebred goldie, but it was so skinny and sad looking he couldn't tell for sure. But its waiflike appearance wasn't the most shocking thing about the poor creature. The dog had horrific burns.

From the back of his head almost to the base of his tail, the dog's handsome golden fur had been burned away. In its place the exposed skin was blistered and weeping, a livid red stripe running the length of his spine.

Appalled by the dog's atrocious injuries, Barry asked what the plan was for him. The animal was clearly in pain, and his burns didn't appear to have been treated. He needed veterinary attention, and he needed it now.

Shelter staff told Barry that the dog was indeed a golden retriever, and was just a year or so old. A woman had found him outside of a Walmart discount store in LA's far northern suburbs. The severity of his injuries meant he was slated for euthanasia, but as a stray the shelter was first required to hold him for several days.

Police were also investigating the matter. The dog's burns were obviously no accident – he had been deliberately tortured. And another dog in the area had been found with similar burns just a week earlier.

When he learned where the dog had been found, Barry understood why the good Samaritan had brought him to the Lancaster shelter, which was quite a drive from where she'd picked him up. He had actually been found in the Antelope Valley in neighbouring Kern County, and in fact there were shelters there that would have been closer.

But Kern County animal shelters were notorious for their high euthanasia rates: in 2010, Kern County's three shelters put to sleep 75 per cent of the animals they took in. This figure has reduced significantly in the years since, but the high-kill reputation persists locally. The lady who found the dog had clearly hoped he might fare better outside of Kern County.

From the look of him, Barry wasn't confident the dog would even live long enough to be put to sleep. But if a kind-hearted stranger had gone to such trouble to give this dog a chance, Barry was determined he would get one.

It looked like he'd be pulling two goldies from the shelter that day.

*

It's not often that people pledge lifelong allegiance to a single breed of dog, but Victor and Anngel Benoun are unashamedly 'goldie people'.

The couple, from Calabasas in LA's San Fernando Valley, brought home their first golden retriever puppy shortly after they married in 1983. His name was Murphy and he lived to be thirteen and a half.

Two more followed, but after they passed away, Victor and Anngel decided to start rescuing goldies rather than purchasing puppies.

In 2006, they adopted a five-year-old named Sammy from SCGRR. Casper the white goldie joined the family just a few months later.

'After we adopted Sammy we told the rescue we'd like him to have a friend. They said they had this dog that was really in trouble, and would we come and take him sight unseen,' says Anngel.

Casper was in terrible shape, Victor recalls. 'He had been terribly abused. He was bred to be a show dog, but we were told he carried the epilepsy gene and had been kept in a cage for two and a half years,' he says. 'He wasn't housebroken. He didn't know how to eat out of a bowl. I had to feed him by hand for several weeks.'

With their patient care and attention, the mistreated and neglected dog transformed from essentially a wild animal to a loving – and beloved – family member. Watching Casper blossom was a profound lesson in the power of love for Victor and Anngel. Just as their focus had previously shifted from puppies to older dogs in need of homes, now they became passionate about saving the dogs that had been most cruelly let down by humans.

Sadly, Sammy passed away in August 2015, but with Casper still thriving at home they weren't necessarily thinking about adding another goldie to their pack just yet. That all changed when they sat down to watch the news one evening in August.

'One of the reporters at our local NBC affiliate does a lot of dog stories and typically they're awfully sad and we can't watch them – we have to change the channel,' says Anngel. 'For some reason, this one we had to watch. We couldn't take our eyes off it. It was like this dog's eyes went through the screen to us.'

The story, covered by reporter Robert Kovacik, was about a golden retriever rescued by SCGRR after sustaining third-degree burns. It was the dog Barry Jacobs had pulled from the Lancaster shelter, after waiting in line for three hours to secure his release.

SCGRR founder Barbara Gale told the news channel the dog was 'very, very scared and confused' and had suffered a seizure after coming into their care. They had named him Fergus, a Scots Gaelic name meaning 'vigour' or 'force'.

Fergus was finally receiving treatment for his burns, which veterinarians at the Animal Medical Center (AMC) in West LA had determined were caused by battery acid being poured down his back. They suspected Fergus's head had been the target, but the corrosive fluid spilled down his back when he tried to get away. There was absolutely no doubt his wounds had been deliberately inflicted.

What was in doubt, however, was whether Fergus would even survive.

Almost immediately after watching the news report, Anngel picked up the phone and called Barbara.

'We'd rescued Sammy and Casper from them so we thought, *Okay, maybe we have the inside track on Fergus*,' she says. 'I said to Barbara, "We just lost our Sammy and we want to adopt Fergus."'

But it wasn't going to be that simple. Fergus's terrible tale had gone viral – it was picked up by media outlets across the US and around the world. SCGRR received more than 500 adoption applications for him from as far afield as Australia and Europe.

Even after the applications were whittled down and Victor and Anngel made the shortlist, they still had to go through the usual application process – including a home check – to ensure they could provide the best possible home for Fergus.

At last, about a month after their initial enquiry, Barbara called again.

'When I'd first called Barbara and said we wanted Fergus she said, "We don't even know if he's going to survive." When she called back she went through all the things that were going to be required, including returning to the vet for multiple laser treatments and more surgery,' says Anngel.

'I was going, "Okay, none of this is scary," and eventually Barbara said, "I guess I always knew he was going to be yours." I just started sobbing. Then I called Victor and said, "Do you want to go meet Fergus?" and he was ecstatic.'

Though they'd been fully briefed about his condition and the extent of his injuries, Victor and Anngel were still shocked when they met Fergus for the first time in the AMC vet hospital.

'At first we weren't sure he was a golden retriever because he resembled a coyote. He was so drawn in the face and so bony. He was down to about twenty kilograms and he should have been about thirty-five kilograms, so he desperately needed to put on weight,' she says.

His emaciated condition led Anngel to suspect Fergus had been a stray for some time before he was attacked, rather than a recently lost or dumped pet. And there was something else that suggested Fergus had been on his own for quite a while: he moos!

'Kern County is cow country and I think he had to have either lived near cows, or when he was a stray he was around cows, because he has the cutest, deep-throated mooing sound when he gets really excited,' she says. 'When people hear it for the first time they go, "What was *that*?"'

Less than a week after he was found on the streets, he started receiving laser therapy to heal the severely damaged tissue on his back. When the Benouns were finally able to bring him home on 22 September, after two months in hospital, Fergus had to wear a t-shirt for six months to protect his healing burns.

In the first eighteen months in his new home, Fergus gained almost ten kilograms of muscle thanks to the gourmet meals Victor and Anngel prepare for him.

Four years on, his fur has mostly grown back, but the follicles and nerves were so badly injured in some areas that a few patches will never fully heal. The skin is thin and fragile and requires constant vigilance.

Anngel says Fergus is unfazed by his unusual appearance. 'Everywhere he was burned there's a white stripe and it's really so cute,' she says. 'He wears his challenge on his back. It's his badge of honour.'

The couple was concerned that his horrific physical ordeal may have negatively impacted his mental health – but quickly discovered Fergus has an indomitable spirit.

'My concern was that he'd be worried about meeting people, but he came right up to us and was in our arms in seconds,' says Victor.

He wasn't entirely emotionally unscathed, though. 'He sleeps in my arms and for the first few months he would have night terrors. When a dog dreams it's kind of cute, but these were true night terrors,' Anngel says. 'I knew that he knew he was finally home and comfortable when he stopped having them.'

AMC vet Dr Alan Schulman told NBC LA that Fergus won over the entire hospital staff with his cheerful approach to life.

'The fact that this guy still trusts people, wags his tail and will let us treat him, considering the horrendous way that some person hurt him, is absolutely remarkable,' Dr Schulman said. 'I'd be the first one to line up and hold that person down and pour whatever chemical he poured on this dog right over him.'

Fergus's injuries were similar to those of six other dogs in the same area, including a Cavalier King Charles Spaniel and several pit bulls, leading police to suspect a single twisted attacker was responsible. The LA County Mayor even offered a $25 000 reward for information leading to an arrest, fearing that a serial animal abuser could escalate to harming people.

To Victor and Anngel's knowledge, however, nobody was ever arrested in connection with the attacks on Fergus or the other dogs, two of which had to be euthanised.

That Fergus survived and recovered from such a horrendous act of cruelty is remarkable – but what he did next was even better.

Fergus became a therapy dog for burns survivors.

Given the national and global interest in Fergus's story, Victor and Anngel were inundated with requests for updates about their resilient retriever.

When Victor set up a Facebook page, Fergus Golden Retriever Survivor, to allow people to track his recovery, he never imagined the path it would lead the couple and their dog down.

He is regularly contacted by other dog owners whose pets have been burned, and is grateful to be in a position to offer them solace and advice.

'Someone from Canada contacted me recently in tears to say their dog had been burned and wanting me to help. I'm not a vet, but I was able to tell them what we went through,' he says.

Fergus has also become quite the celebrity. He appeared on television with high-profile dog trainer Cesar Millan and evangelical pastor T.D. Jakes. 'He's really helped spread the word against animal violence,' says Victor.

Soon after Fergus came home to Calabasas, Victor received a message from a nurse at the LA County + USC Medical Center burns unit. She said the staff had been so inspired by Fergus's story they wanted to contribute to his ongoing veterinary costs.

Victor and Anngel were so touched by the gesture they asked if they could bring Fergus to the hospital to meet the team.

'We took Fergus down there and met some of the most incredible people in the world. They were complete strangers, and yet they had raised a thousand dollars for him,' he says.

Fergus quickly became the burns unit's unofficial mascot, and when he passed his Canine Good Citizen test in October 2017 he became its first therapy dog. He regularly visits the unit and spends time with patients of all ages and at various stages of their burns recovery journey.

'In some cases it's hard to tell if the patient is male or female because their injuries are so severe. The nurses tell us they can be belligerent because they're so angry about what happened to them, but they see Fergus and they smile,' says Anngel.

'It's a really nice thing in particular when the children see him. They think it will never be okay, and then they see what he overcame. We see some pretty desperate people, but after they see Fergus their outlook is very different.'

Victor finds it hard to put into words precisely what it is that Fergus does for the people he meets. He can't speak, obviously, but he seems to have an innate understanding of what the hospital patients have been through. They seem to recognise something in each other.

'People say it's unconditional love, but it's not even that – there's just no judgement. Burns survivors tend to have their guards up. They're afraid to let anybody in,' he says. 'But Fergus went through this too, so now they're with somebody who's kin. You ought to see the defence mechanisms just drop away. He really does help them.'

Over time, Fergus's role has expanded and he now visits dementia and trauma patients at various facilities as well.

He also works with and attends events for a range of other groups, including children who have autism, literacy programs where children read to dogs, the accessible playground Brandon's Village and Ronald McDonald House.

'He's very busy – I'm just his valet,' Victor laughs. 'He loves going out and being part of everything.'

In summer 2018, Fergus was invited to visit Camp Arroyo, a northern California camp for children with chronic medical conditions, developmental disabilities and youth at-risk run by The Taylor Family Foundation. Some of the campers are burns survivors.

'It was a six-hour drive, but it was so touching to watch these kids. There was one little girl who came up to us after she had requested a private conversation with us and Fergus,' says Anngel. 'She wanted to tell us that she was exactly like him, that she had finally found someone she could relate to.'

Fergus's connection with people really does seem to transcend the limits of human–canine communication. 'There's something magical about this dog. Until you see him, it's difficult to fully grasp,' says Victor.

Fergus is around five years old now, and his life today is a world away from its terrifying beginnings. While he has some ongoing issues with his wounds, and still has occasional seizures, there is no evidence to suggest his injuries will shorten his life.

Victor and Anngel don't think Fergus has forgotten what happened to him; rather, he has made a conscious choice not to let it hold him back.

'Sometimes when I'm cuddling him I'll look into his eyes and say, "I sure wish you could tell me what happened to you,"' she says. 'No one will ever know exactly what happened to Fergus, but I'm glad it's not in his memory.'

But while there's no doubt he is a happy, secure dog these days, the scars on his back serve as a constant reminder of what he went through.

'I'm thrilled with how happy and well adjusted he is now, but it's hard not to think about it. There's a lot of abused animals in this world and it's really just tragic,' says Victor.

Their experience with Fergus has not only reaffirmed the Benouns' personal commitment to providing a loving home for dogs, it has made them vocal advocates of rescue and responsible pet ownership in general.

It can be frustrating when even people who have observed Fergus's recovery up close say they would never rescue a dog.

'We have friends who just don't believe in rescue because they don't want to "inherit" problems. To that I say you don't know what you're getting with a puppy either,' Anngel says.

'A dog has to know the minute they come into your house that it's their forever home. Whether you pay for a puppy or you rescue a senior, you have to make the commitment: that dog stays with you forever. Period.'

To Victor and Anngel, a dog's origins are irrelevant – it's the security of their permanent home that makes all the difference.

'Animals need attention, love and to know they're secure – just like people do. I think the mistake a lot of people make is they look at them like stuffed animals, like they don't have feelings or emotions,' he says. 'Being insecure is one of the worst things for a dog. It's a matter of being consistent and being kind.'

On Boxing Day in 2018, Fergus's canine brother, Casper, sadly passed away just shy of his thirteenth birthday. Less than a week later, Anngel and Victor decided to open their hearts to another goldie in need.

Frodo was on his way to the US from Turkey, where he had originally been the resident dog at a pharmaceutical company. When the company changed hands, the new owners didn't like dogs – so they left Frodo chained to a kennel for a year.

The three-year-old pooch arrived in California in January and fit right into the family.

'Frodo's biggest issue was that he didn't speak English – all his commands were in Turkish, so we had to teach him,' says Victor.

Just like his big brother, Frodo looks set to have a fulfilling life as a therapy dog. As well as continuing to work with burns survivors, Victor and Anngel would like to work with military veterans.

'Fergus took a long time to pass his Canine Good Citizen test – in fact we weren't sure if he would ever pass – but Frodo passed his on the first try,' he says. 'He's going to be a little therapy dog star.'

In the future, the couple hopes to adopt senior goldies. It's a heartbreaking fact that shelters are full of dogs abandoned for being 'too old'.

'People surrender their senior dogs either for medical reasons or because they want to get a younger dog,' says Anngel. 'The dog is an equal member of your family and you want to turn Grandma in? It makes me so sad.'

It is undeniably poetic that a dog who survived horrific burns should go on to provide comfort for human burns survivors. But in truth, everything about Fergus's story could have been taken from an epic poem. He faced tremendous odds and he conquered them all, just like the warrior his name connotes.

And best of all, Fergus got his happy ending.

KALU

From a shocking accident to loving life on one leg

It's fair to say that life is tough for dogs and cats in the island nation of Sri Lanka. It is a cruel irony that stray animals are everywhere – there are reportedly three million street dogs alone – and yet pet ownership is uncommon.

Instead of relying on people for a warm bed and a full belly, the homeless creatures that roam Sri Lankan cities and villages risk injury and abuse at the hands of humans every single day. Disease and neglect are the norm. Veterinarians are virtually nonexistent outside of the major cities. Gruesome collisions with cars, trucks and trains barely raise an eyebrow, let alone a rescue effort.

Stray animals are widely demonised, and cruelty is seen by many as justified due to the threat and fear of rabies. Life isn't much more pleasant for dogs that have owners: most are kept as guard dogs, not family pets, and spend their days chained or confined to kennels.

Sri Lanka is a poor country – nearly half the population lives on less than $5 a day – and the culture simply doesn't place much value on the lives of companion animals, says Kim Cooling, who founded the charity Animal SOS Sri Lanka in 2007.

Kim, a former social worker from Essex in the UK, had long felt heartsick over the treatment of the tiny country's animals, so she set about raising money to buy a four-acre parcel of land at Galle on Sri Lanka's southwestern tip.

When she bought it, the land was essentially a jungle. It had no running water or electricity. Along with a team of volunteers, Kim – who runs the charity from the UK but visits Sri Lanka twice a year – slowly developed the land and created all the infrastructure needed to house a permanent population of strays. They dug wells and erected buildings including kennels and shelter areas, as well as an apartment for staff to live in with a clinic downstairs.

In June 2009, Animal SOS Sri Lanka opened its sanctuary. It is now home to more than 1600 free-roaming dogs, and sixty cats housed in a separate cattery. Very occasionally, an animal will be adopted by a local family, but the vast majority of animals – many of which have special needs – will live out their days at the sanctuary.

The charity also aims to educate though its community outreach programs, offering free neutering, spaying and rabies vaccinations, as well as providing emergency veterinary care for sick and injured animals.

It costs about £40 000 per month to feed and house the animals and keep the organisation running. Unwanted puppies and kittens are frequently thrown over the sanctuary's walls, which puts further pressure on its already limited resources.

It is thankless, exhausting and often disheartening work. Some days it feels like each step forward is immediately followed by ten steps back.

But Kim keeps persisting because she believes every animal deserves a chance. That's especially true, she says, of the disabled dogs that would face a slow, painful death without support of the sanctuary.

'We've had paralysed dogs that have walked again after a year at the sanctuary. Without that chance there's no hope,' says Kim. 'As long as they're with people that love them, and they get the care they need, they can have a happy life. We very much believe in that.'

There are also days at the sanctuary that make all the hard graft worthwhile; days when the tears and frustration, the sleepless nights spent worrying about making ends meet, suddenly seem insignificant.

They're the days when the Animal SOS Sri Lanka team witnesses a survival story so remarkable it can only be called a miracle.

The day Kalu arrived was one of those days.

In Sinhala, the native language of Sri Lanka's Sinhalese people, the world 'kalu' means black. Stray dogs in Sri Lanka rarely have names (and if they do they're unlikely to be complimentary), and even those animals that are part of a family are generally named along literal rather than imaginative lines.

Consequently, a disproportionate number of black dogs – as well as black cats and even cattle – that have owners are called Kalu.

But while she may be just one *of* a million dogs that share her name, the Kalu that arrived at Animal SOS Sri Lanka in early September 2017 is one *in* a million in the most remarkable sense.

The day before Kalu arrived, Kim was at home in the Essex suburb of Woodford, attending to charity business. She had spent a long day at the computer and it was already evening when she received a message via the Animal SOS Sri Lanka Facebook page.

It's not unusual for Kim and the staff at the sanctuary to be alerted via email or social media to animals in desperate need of help. In fact, such appeals are depressingly frequent. Every single day, Animal SOS Sri Lanka is inundated with requests for assistance.

This message was different. It was written in Sinhala, which Kim doesn't speak, so she didn't know what it said – but she didn't need to be able to read it. The photograph that accompanied the message spoke a thousand horrifying words.

'Someone sent me this picture and I had to look twice. I couldn't read the message so I didn't know what was going on. I just looked at this photo and thought, *Is this even real?*' she recalls.

The photo showed what looked like a Sinhala Hound – Sri Lanka's indigenous street dog breed – lying on her side in the long grass of a field. Shockingly, three of the dog's legs lay next to her, severed from her body. Only her back right leg remained intact.

It was difficult to tell from the picture whether the dog was even alive. Her eyes were closed, which seemed to suggest the worst. But why would the person who sent the message have bothered to locate and reach out to an animal sanctuary unless they hoped the poor creature could be saved?

Kim has seen a lot of gruesome injuries, but she had never been faced with anything like this. What on earth had happened to this dog? She couldn't imagine such damage resulting from a vehicle accident. Perhaps it was a case of appalling cruelty – could a human being really be responsible for this carnage?

Whatever had occurred, Kim knew she had to act immediately if the dog was somehow still clinging to life. Sri Lanka is five and a half hours ahead of the UK, so it was already well into the night there – she couldn't waste a moment.

Kim quickly got in touch with a Sinhala-speaking contact who also spoke good English. He read the message and explained that the dog's name was Kalu and she lived in Polonnaruwa, around 380 kilometres from the sanctuary in Galle.

Her contact became the go-between for Kim and the people trying to save the dog in Polonnaruwa. Slowly, she was able to piece together Kalu's story.

Kalu was an owned dog, and much loved by her family, who were poor local villagers. She would go with them to temple every day, then spend the rest of her time roaming the village and surrounds.

'She lived freely, which was nice because a lot of owned dogs are caged or chained up their whole lives,' Kim says. 'But Kalu used to follow her owners everywhere.'

Villagers had discovered Kalu in the field first thing that morning. Her family hadn't seen her since the night before, so she had been lying out there, dehydrated, bleeding, alone and in agony, for twelve hours or more. She was also heavily pregnant.

Though nobody could be certain of exactly what had happened to Kalu, the most likely scenario was that she had been run over by a harvester machine whose driver simply hadn't seen her amid the long grass. Harvesters have sharp blades for cutting crops such as maize and soybean.

Kalu may well have been napping in the field, and when woken by the machine, simply couldn't move her swollen body from its path in time.

Kim felt more astonished as each awful new fact came to light. 'I couldn't believe that she had even survived the night after having three legs chopped off. How she didn't bleed to death or die of shock I don't know,' she says.

It really is a mystery. If the machine had severed her legs cleanly or 'surgically', the uncontrolled haemorrhage from the wounds would quickly have claimed Kalu's life. Her pregnancy should have complicated the situation because her body would have been pumping extra blood into the placenta and foetuses, meaning there was less to go around. And yet, somehow, she did not bleed to death. One possible explanation is that the harvester first crushed Kalu's legs, compressing the veins and arteries and effectively sealing them, preventing further blood loss.

It might have helped if it had been cold that night: cooling the body slows down the metabolism and can help to stabilise a critically injured patient. But that doesn't seem to have been a factor in Kalu's case either. While the hours of darkness are obviously cooler than the daytime, Sri Lanka is warm all year round, with temperatures still hovering around 25°C even at night.

Each hour that ticked by should have increased the risk of potentially deadly infection taking hold in her wounds – but it didn't.

Put simply, there is absolutely no medical reason why pregnant Kalu should have survived such catastrophic injuries at all, let alone for an entire night in a field.

But she did. And the fact of that survival inspired what happened next.

Kalu's owners were distraught when news of their beloved dog's disastrous predicament reached them. There are no veterinarians anywhere near Polonnaruwa, but even if there were, what could possibly be done for a pregnant dog that has lost three of her four legs? The family couldn't even afford pain-relieving medication for her, let alone major medical intervention.

Long-term survival seemed unlikely, and surviving with any quality of life seemed impossible. The villagers came to a sad consensus: Kalu should be euthanised as soon as possible.

Then came her second reprieve.

'They were going to "put her out of her misery", but the owners loved her a lot. They looked at her face and just couldn't do it,' Kim says. 'Instead, they all rallied around to help her. It was a herculean effort, but the whole village got behind this dog in a country where dogs are not always treated well.'

A local man known to have an affinity with animals was summoned to the field. He performed rudimentary surgery, sewing up her wounds right then and there. They weren't cleaned or sterilised, and Kalu received no anaesthetic, but they were at least closed.

'In these remote areas they don't have any vets, but this guy was known for being good with wildlife. He stitched up her wounds very coarsely. It was awful – there were bits of grass and hay in the wounds – but our vet said it basically saved her life,' she says.

Then the community collectively searched for somewhere they could take Kalu, or someone that could at least advise them on what to do next. It took time, but in yet another incredible stroke of luck, they found the one place on the island that has never turned its back on an animal in need.

After hours of to-ing and fro-ing, Kim at last had the complete story. Without hesitation, she typed three words to her contact in Sri Lanka.

We'll take her.

Then she alerted the sanctuary's onsite managers to the imminent arrival of a pregnant, traumatised, one-legged dog.

'They could not believe it. They said, "Is she going to survive?" I didn't know but I said, "Just let her come and we'll figure it out,"' she says. 'She was in a field with no real help. We would assess the situation and do our best for her.'

But first they had to actually get Kalu to the sanctuary. It was already past midnight in Sri Lanka, more than twelve hours after Kalu was discovered in the field and up to twenty-four hours since her injury. Polonnaruwa is at least a seven-hour drive from Galle. It was astounding that she had made it this far – could she hang on a little longer?

The villagers were determined to try. They gently loaded Kalu onto the back of a rickety old truck and headed south. Ten thousand kilometres away in England, Kim knew she wouldn't sleep that night.

'I coordinated her rescue all night. I was sending messages to my contact saying, *Is she still alive? Get them to wrap her up, get them to give her some water*,' she says.

The mood at the sanctuary was apprehensive as manager Marie Bechsen Hansen and staff awaited Kalu's arrival. They only had thirdhand information about her condition, and didn't have any real idea what was in store. They weren't convinced she would even be alive when she reached the sanctuary.

Early in the morning, the truck rattled up to the sanctuary gates. What they saw when they peeked into the back was more shocking than they could have imagined.

Kalu was not only alive, she was *happy*.

'When she arrived she had a smile on her face. We didn't know what to expect with Kalu – we thought this was going to be one of our worst cases. We all thought she'd be in terrible pain and half dead,' says Kim. 'She really shocked us. For her to arrive with a smile was incredible. The sanctuary staff looked at her and said, "She wants a chance."'

If Kalu wanted to live, Kim and her team would do everything they could to help her.

The first thing they did was re-open the stitching of her stumps, flush out and clean her wounds and then properly suture them. It was a painful procedure that would usually be performed under general anaesthetic, but Kalu could only be lightly sedated because the veterinary team wasn't sure whether her unborn puppies were still alive. If they were, anaesthesia could kill them.

Unsurprisingly, Kalu bore the surgery with the stoicism that was fast becoming her trademark.

She was also given pain relief and intravenous antibiotics to try to ward off infection. 'We were very worried about her getting sepsis because her stumps were so dirty,' Kim explains.

After that, the team could do nothing but wait. Any further decisions about Kalu's future were put on hold until sanctuary staff could tell whether or not her puppies had survived the ordeal.

'We didn't know how far along she was with her pregnancy because we don't have a [powerful] scanner. We saw the puppies in there, but it was very hard to tell whether they were dead or alive,' she says. 'We just had to bide our time to see what was happening.'

Sadly, they got their answer just a few days later.

'Kalu started to produce a lot of foul-smelling discharge and we realised we'd have to do a caesarean straight away. Sadly, the puppies didn't make it, and it looked like they'd died at the time of the accident, whether from the shock or the accident itself we don't know.'

So Kalu was now not only recovering from the accident that claimed three of her legs, she also had to cope with caesarean surgery and the loss of her litter.

Like humans, dogs can experience depression, but if Kalu was mourning the loss of her puppies or her mobility, it didn't show.

'She rose through it all. She was bright and perky and always had a smile on her face,' says Kim. 'She's an amazing dog. We see life and death stories every day, but Kalu really stands out.'

Later, she needed further surgery on one of her stumps, but once again she bounced back quickly. No sooner had her stitches healed, Kalu was figuring out her own unique method of getting around her new home.

'Marie left her out in the lounge area one night and the next morning she heard Kalu knocking her head against the bedroom door wanting to be let in,' Kim laughs. 'She gets around on her one leg like a little seal.'

Two years on, Kalu is thriving. She has also become well known both locally and internationally. She has her own Instagram account with a growing following (@kaluthewonderdog), and posts about her on the Animal SOS Sri Lanka Facebook page always attract hundreds of likes and comments. In early 2018 she was even featured on the Animal Planet TV series *Evan Goes Wild*, starring celebrity US vet Dr Evan Antin.

'People come from all over Sri Lanka to see her. They come to the sanctuary gate and say, "Can we meet Kalu?"' says Kim. 'She's very famous. Everyone has just embraced her.'

Tenacious as she is, Kalu can't stay outside with hundreds of free-roaming dogs, so she lives in the manager's apartment. And arguably nobody has embraced Kalu more completely than sanctuary manager Marie, who adores the feisty pooch. According to Kim, the feeling is mutual.

'Marie has been there for Kalu right from the start. When she has a couple of days off and comes back to the sanctuary, Kalu screams with joy to see her,' she says. 'Kalu is so intelligent and so loved.'

Animal SOS Sri Lanka is well known for its 'Cart Gang': a pack of paralysed dogs that zoom around the sanctuary in their wheeled carts. The first disabled dog the charity ever took in, Hope, is still thriving there nine years later. People often ask why Kalu doesn't use a cart, and the answer is simple – she doesn't want one!

'We did get her a cart but she doesn't like it. She looked at us like, *You're mad – you know I can get around! I don't need this, take it off me*,' Kim laughs. 'She gets around in her own way. We've got puppies in the apartment and one was pulling Kalu's tail and she chased it all around the apartment. She has her likes and dislikes, and she doesn't take any nonsense.'

Nor does Kim, especially the sort of nonsense that comes from ill-informed people who claim dogs like Kalu can't possibly have any quality of life and should be euthanised. Everyone who knows Kalu – and the dozens of dogs like her at the sanctuary – knows such a negative perspective couldn't be further from the truth.

'People say, "How can a dog like that be happy?" but she is. She's coped very well with her disability and she's happy to be alive,' says Kim. 'She's a brave dog, and a very big part of what we do, which is to give a chance to animals that wouldn't otherwise get one. She very much wanted to live.

'Kalu was very lucky to come to us. I don't think she'd be alive if she'd gone anywhere else in Sri Lanka.'

The Animal SOS Sri Lanka ethos is entirely about putting the animal first. It doesn't matter what people might think about a dog's appearance or abilities. The question is always the same: what is the right thing to do *for the dog?*

'A lot of people don't want to see an "eyesore" of a dog that has a disability, but we look at the point of view of the animal,' she says. 'Disability does impact life, but it's not the end of life. Special needs animals do need more attention, but if they have quality of life, they deserve a chance.

'There is no reason to end the life of a dog with a disability just because it's disabled. I don't believe we have the right to do that. We have a lot of Western vets volunteer here and they come in saying, "These dogs can't be happy." But they leave saying, "They *are* happy – it's changed my mindset."'

Kalu has no ongoing health issues as a result of her accident. She is fastidiously clean, toileting outside and then scooting herself away. When she's not supervising the canine residents of the manager's apartment or hanging out in the downstairs office with Marie, Kalu enjoys rolling around on the grass and visiting the nearby beach to splash around in the shallows.

She is about eight years old now and will spend the rest of her life at the sanctuary. Kim says there was never any question that Kalu would stay; loved though she was in her village, her former owners simply don't have the means to meet her needs. They do follow her progress on Facebook, however, and Kim understands the whole village is proud of how well the brave dog is doing.

There is certainly something magical about Kalu's amazing survival, but equally miraculous in Kim's mind is the fact that so many people came together to help her in a country where the prevailing attitude towards animal welfare could be called indifferent at best.

Kim regularly receives calls from locals who won't even take an injured puppy inside for safekeeping when it's dying at their front door. That the people of Polonnaruwa went to such lengths for a dog that most people would have concluded stood no chance of survival is something she finds enormously moving.

'Those villagers are very, very poor, but they drove all night and turned up here with this dog in this ramshackle truck. For a village to come together like that really choked me up,' she says. 'I was very shocked and humbled and I actually thought there was hope.'

But while it literally took a village to save Kalu, the true miracle is of course the little dog herself. Medically speaking, her survival is unfathomable, but if spirit, grit and pure iron will count for anything, it's not surprising at all that Kalu made it through.

Kim puts it best: 'She lost her puppies and she lost three of her legs, but she never lost her spirit.'

GUY

From friendless shelter dog to rubbing shoulders with royalty

The small town of Mount Sterling, Kentucky, has that sepia-toned Main Street, USA, kind of vibe. An hour's drive from the state capital, Frankfort, its wide downtown streets are lined with historic buildings and well-kept shopfronts, while the leafy residential neighbourhoods offer neat lawns and homes with wraparound porches. Among its most notable attractions are historic churches, a civil war monument and a collection of stately properties built by wealthy settlers.

Beyond the Mount Sterling city limits, much of Montgomery County – and indeed much of the state of Kentucky – is distinctly rural: hilly and densely wooded, dotted with creeks and lakes, and boasting vastly more trees than people.

Out here, hunting is arguably the most popular recreational pursuit. There are more than 350 000 licensed

hunters in Kentucky. The largest elk herd east of the Missis-
sippi River calls Kentucky home, as do almost a million
deer. There is a growing bear population, as well as
squirrels, rabbits, quail, ducks and even cranes.

Where there are hunters, there are hunting dogs – and
it's here that Mount Sterling's genteel façade slips to reveal a
darker reality. Hunters tend to prefer hound dog breeds
including beagles, mountain curs and treeing walker
coonhounds, with individual shooters often owning a dozen
dogs or more. The hunting season for most large animals
runs from the start of September until the end of December;
the small game season runs until February. And when the
season ends, hundreds of hounds are simply abandoned.

In Montgomery County, as in all of Kentucky and indeed
across the south-eastern US, there is an entrenched culture
of dumping unwanted dogs deep in the woods where the
chances are they will never be found. Many are old, some
are sick, injured or malnourished. All have been deemed
surplus to requirements and left to fend for themselves as
they wander the remote backroads.

As a result, local rescue groups and county-run animal
shelters, stretched to breaking point at the best of times, are
flooded with surrendered and dumped hound dogs at
the same time every year.

Shelters are constantly at capacity, adoption rates are
low, and most have no choice but to put healthy animals to
sleep to make room for more. Those quick to euthanise are
known as 'high-kill' shelters. No-kill shelters – those that
will keep an animal its entire life if necessary – are virtually

nonexistent in the south. Researchers at the University of Tennessee estimate that overcrowded shelters in the southeast put to death at least 80 per cent of their animals every year.

Often the only hope for these discarded dogs is a ticket to ride: transport north to a less congested shelter or rescue group.

The idea of relocating dogs from southern shelters first took hold in the aftermath of Hurricane Katrina in 2005. As animal rescuers moved thousands of pets out of the devastation in New Orleans, they forged strong partnerships with their counterparts above the Mason–Dixon line, the historic unofficial border between north and south.

The practice continued, and today some southern shelters send up to 1000 dogs a year to the northern US and Canada. Sometimes the animals are loaded en masse onto enormous transport trucks, but more often than not they travel in small groups in a sort of human chain of volunteer drivers. Each driver travels for an hour or so to a designated drop spot, where the dogs are loaded into the next vehicle to continue their journey to safety – and so on and so on.

It's a labour-intensive undertaking that not only requires military-style organisation and precision, but also dozens of people willing to give up their time to drive long distances. It is far from the ideal option, but for most of these hapless hounds it's the only option. Not one of them is truly safe until they're on the freeway, heading north.

Into this dicey predicament wandered a bedraggled beagle in January 2015. Like so many others, he'd been found alone and scared in the woods near Mount Sterling as hunting season drew to a close.

The dog wasn't in great shape. He was somewhere between one and three years old, but instead of the boundless energy and robust constitution a hound of his age should have had, he was filthy, painfully thin and downcast. He weighed just 7 kilograms – a fully-grown male beagle should weigh about 11 kilograms. His enormous brown eyes could only be described as haunted.

Perhaps he somehow knew what lay ahead. The beagle was taken to the jam-packed Montgomery County Animal Shelter in Mount Sterling, where every dog is essentially on death row at that time of year. In the unlikely event he was simply lost, not dumped, and had an owner frantically searching for him, they had just a day or two to find him and take him home.

The possibility that he might be adopted quickly was almost laughable; shelter traffic in Kentucky in January was decidedly one way.

No, this dog's remaining time would almost certainly be short. Unless someone remarkable stepped in to offer him a lifeline, he would be euthanised alongside dozens of others.

He needed someone willing to move heaven and earth to give him a second chance.

Someone like Dolores Doherty.

There's an old adage that goes something like this: If you want a job done, ask a busy person to do it.

It's quite possible the saying was inspired by Dolores Doherty.

Dolores is the proverbial plate spinner: she has a million and one things on the go at any given moment, but she's never too busy to help someone in need – especially if that someone has four legs and is all out of options.

She grew up with beagles and adores the breed. But there was one childhood dog in particular that would change the course of Dolores's life in ways she never could have anticipated.

'I had a little dog named Tippy as a child. He was my little friend and I used to dress him up in my doll clothes,' she recalls.

Tragically, Tippy became sick and died before his time, and his loss lit a fire within Dolores that still burns brightly today. To her, the beagle is simply the perfect dog.

'There's so much negative publicity around beagles because of their involvement with hunting, but they don't dig and they don't bark,' she says. 'They do well in apartments. They're a really good breed for many people.'

She and husband Jim have rarely been without a beagle by their side in thirty-eight years of marriage. Then, in the noughties, Dolores became involved with a Kentucky-based rescue group that transported beagles from various shelters there to new lives in her home province of Ontario, Canada.

When she realised the extent of the beagle dumping problem in the southern US, she says, she just couldn't turn her back.

'If a hunter has thirty dogs and a couple don't come back from a hunt, it's not a big deal to them. Or if they're not good hunting dogs, they'll kick them to the corner,' she says. 'They feel the animals are there for them to use, and when they no longer need them they can get rid of them. A dog is a disposable thing: it's not a pet and they don't have a lot of emotion for the animal. A lot of dogs are on chains for their entire lives. It's really very sad. The attitude to animals here in Canada is a little different.'

In 2010, after a long career in financial planning, Dolores retired and decided the time was right to do even more for her beloved breed.

'I had been transporting dogs on one of the legs of the transports since 2004. I'd drive them for about an hour and then hand the dogs over to the next driver. All of the dogs were going to wonderful rescues, and when I retired I had the time so I thought, *I can take a couple of dogs and find them a home,*' she says.

But it was never going to be just 'a couple' of dogs. When word of her offer reached Kentucky, Dolores found herself in high demand. 'When the rescue found out they said, "Take them, take them" and all of a sudden I had about thirty beagles!'

Many people would feel daunted by such a mammoth undertaking, but Dolores channelled her stress into decisive action. She set herself up as an official rescue, choosing the name A Dog's Dream in honour of Tippy. She taught herself to list adoptable dogs on Petfinder.com, the largest pet adoption website in North America. And she figured out how to coordinate vet checks and finalise paperwork for dozens of dogs before they even left Kentucky.

'The shelters will email me pictures of dogs they have that they think I might like. The volunteers that I work with will pull the dogs out of the shelter and get them into a vet to be taken care of,' she explains.

It was a steep learning curve to say the least.

'I was just going to do it as a hobby, but it's become a full-time job. It's 24/7 and it's really demanding. My house is full of dog beds and dogs. We're always tripping over dogs,' says Dolores. 'Fortunately I had a lot of help from other rescues to guide me.'

The dogs that arrived from the Kentucky shelters were often in poor condition, both physically and emotionally. Dolores says the grim shelter environment takes a significant mental toll on even the most effervescent hounds.

'I don't know of any dog that does well in a shelter. They're thrown into a small cage with a cement floor and no bed. It's like jail,' she says. 'Their food is thrown to them. They clean the kennels with high pressure hoses. They get no exercise, no love. There's a lot of dogs, so there's barking constantly. Often dogs are euthanised and the ones that are left know.'

One thing Dolores didn't need to worry about was a dearth of homes for the imported dogs. She lives in the heart of Ontario's 'Golden Horseshoe' region, a 31 000-square-kilometre swathe that starts at Niagara Falls and wraps around the western end of Lake Ontario before turning north-east to Toronto and ending at Oshawa.

It is the most densely populated and industrialised region in Canada, with more than nine million inhabitants, many of whom live in high-density housing such as apartment towers or homes without backyards.

In other words, Dolores lives at the centre of a universe in which beagles are ideal pets.

'They just came in one door and went out the other – they were adopted so quickly. They are a breed that's good for both kids and older people. People also use them as therapy dogs,' she says. 'There's such a big market for them where I live. I have a huge audience, and it's a good one. Many people come back and want a second one.'

As A Dog's Dream became well known, Dolores became adept at running adoption events. These are popular across North America because they are a one-stop shop for anybody looking to adopt a dog. Few small rescues have shelters, instead housing the dogs in their care in a network of foster homes; adoption events bring all their adoptable animals together in one place.

In January 2015, she was preparing for the herculean task of bringing about twenty dogs from different homes to an event on the outskirts of Toronto when she got a call from Kentucky.

It was a volunteer at the Montgomery County Animal Shelter in Mount Sterling. They had a sad, scared little beagle that needed a one-way ticket off the euthanasia list. He didn't have a name yet: shelter staff had dubbed him 'little guy' due to his diminutive stature.

The sight of the dog's huge, doleful eyes struck Dolores

74

right in the heart. 'They showed me pictures of him and I said, "Oh my goodness, with those eyes? Of course I will!"'

And so the wheels were set in motion to spring the beagle from the shelter and transport him to Canada, where Dolores was certain he would have a wonderful new life.

She didn't have time to imagine just how wonderful, because while she waited for her new arrival – he tested positive for heartworm and spent two months being treated at a Kentucky vet – Dolores had preparations for the March adoption event and the day-to-day running of A Dog's Dream to be getting on with.

She is fastidious about doing her due diligence with all prospective adopters. Everyone must complete a detailed application form and provide references, and she tries to conduct home visits where possible to verify that the adopter's property is suitable for a beagle.

In the days before the adoption event, Dolores received an email from a woman who said she wanted to adopt a beagle as a companion for her resident dog. As she always does, Dolores sent back the standard A Dog's Dream application form.

'Within ten minutes she had filled it out and sent it back to me,' she says. 'It was unusual. People don't usually respond that quickly.'

This lady was clearly *really* keen on becoming a beagle parent. Dolores looked at the residential address on the form: it was just west of downtown Toronto. The adoption event would be held at a pet store in Milton, at least a

45-minute drive into the suburbs and probably too far to expect an adopter to trek on a Sunday.

But Dolores sent the event details to the woman anyway. If she was that eager to adopt, perhaps she would be willing to make the trip.

Dolores returned to her administrative duties, the woman's name already fading from memory as a hundred more pressing tasks clamoured for attention.

It was a name that would soon be on everybody's lips.

It is difficult now to remember a time when Meghan Markle wasn't a household name, but here's a potted history for those few uninitiated.

Born Rachel Meghan Markle in Los Angeles, California, Meghan is today best known as the Duchess of Sussex, the divorced former actress who married Prince Harry in May 2018. In May 2019, the couple welcomed their first child, Archie Harrison Mountbatten-Windsor.

But before she became a member of the British royal family, Meghan grew up in Hollywood, where from an early age she dreamed of being an actress. Her father, Thomas Markle, was an Emmy-winning director of photography and lighting director on the daytime soap opera *General Hospital* and sitcom *Married . . . with Children*, and Meghan was a regular visitor to the set. In fact, her first TV appearance was a small role as a nurse in *General Hospital*.

Meghan made brief appearances in a range of TV shows and films before landing her big break in 2011: the role of paralegal-turned-attorney Rachel Zane in the USA Network show *Suits*. She filmed seven seasons of the popular show.

Suits is filmed in Toronto, and Meghan lived there for nine months of the year, renting a house in the quiet, family-oriented neighbourhood of Seaton Village.

When Meghan's first marriage to actor and producer Trevor Engelson ended in 2013, she decided the time was right to adopt her first dog. She recounted the story of how she came to adopt her Labrador–shepherd mix, Bogart, to Canada's *Best Health* magazine in 2016.

'I was in LA and I went to this dog rescue and they had gotten him and his brother. They found them in an alley in this neighbourhood called Downey at five weeks old,' she told the publication. 'So I saw him and I was sitting there with him and then Ellen DeGeneres and Portia de Rossi walk in. Now, I don't know her, but Ellen goes, "Is that your dog?" And I said, "No," and she's like, "You have to take that dog." And I said, "Well, I'm deciding."' And she's like, "Rescue the dog!"'

As it turned out, talk show host Ellen is very persuasive. 'It's sort of like if Oprah tells you to do something. I'm sitting there holding him and she's like, "Have you thought of a name for him yet?" And I said, "Well, I think I'd name him Bogart," and she's like, "You're taking the dog home,"' Meghan said.

'And she walks outside to get into her car, but instead of getting in she turns around and comes and taps on the window glass and she yells, "Take the dog!" And so I brought him home. Because Ellen told me to.'

Meghan had had Bogart for about two years when she decided in 2015 that he could use a friend. 'I started to see that he loves the company of people, but just like I love the company of dogs, I don't want to be around solely dogs all day long so I realised he might like to have a companion,' she told *Best Health*.

Her online sleuthing led her to A Dog's Dream and Dolores Doherty's inbox. Dolores had never seen an episode of *Suits*, so she didn't recognise the name of its lead actress when she read her email.

Nor did she recognise the striking young lady who approached her at the Pet Valu store in Milton on the day of the adoption event. It was only when the future royal introduced herself that Dolores put two and two together and realised she was the same woman that had returned her application form so promptly the week before.

'She actually did show up. She was short and petite and she had on sweats and her hair up in a black ski cap. She had no makeup on and she's just beautiful,' she says. 'She was a pretty normal person.'

Meghan had brought a male companion with her: her Labrador mix, Bogart. She wanted him to have the final say in choosing his new best friend. The first beagle to pique her interest was a male called Roman.

'He was a very beautiful dog, but Roman and Bogart didn't seem to hit it off. They didn't pay much attention to each other,' says Dolores.

Undeterred, Meghan continued to meet the beagles available for adoption. That's when she spotted the latest addition to the A Dog's Dream family: the petite beagle newly arrived from Mount Sterling.

It was a remarkable stroke of luck that 'the little guy' was even at the event that day. Now healthy and heartworm negative, he was so fresh off the proverbial boat that he hadn't even been in Canada for a full day.

'One of my volunteers was holding him, because these events are pretty scary for the dogs and we want to make them feel better. Meghan saw him and said, "I want that one,"' Dolores recalls. 'I said, "If they get along that's fine with me."'

The volunteer set the dog down and he and Bogart immediately made a beeline for each other. All the signs were encouraging.

'They were nuzzling each other and wagging their tails and sniffing in tandem. We could see that they were friends,' she says.

While Bogart and the beagle whose paperwork still listed him as 'the little guy' got to know each other, Dolores chatted with Meghan.

'She was already quite famous for her role in *Suits*, but I had no idea who she was. I asked her what she did and she said she worked in the film industry,' she says. 'In Toronto there's a huge film industry and it employs a lot of people. She didn't say anything more, so I didn't know if she was a set decorator or something else.'

With the dogs' mutual affection for each other obvious, Meghan asked to officially adopt 'the little guy'. While Dolores was happy for her to take Bogart's new friend home that day, there were still some formalities to sort out.

It was the first inkling Dolores had that Meghan might not be just a regular dog owner.

'I said I'd have to come and do a home visit and she said, "That's fine, just give me some time so I can make an appointment for you with my security people,"' she says. 'I needed a reference and she gave me three referees to call. She was never, "I'm Meghan Markle, I don't have to do all that." Anything I asked, she did. She was very nice and she paid the adoption fee in cash.'

Dolores never did make it to Seaton Village to carry out a home check on Meghan's property. She didn't need to. The day after she took her new canine companion home, the future duchess started posting pictures of him on her now deleted Instagram account.

'After he appeared on her Instagram I started getting these emails from people saying, "You adopted a dog to Meghan Markle!" I said, "Who is she?" I had no idea,' she says. 'I hadn't adopted a dog to a celebrity before. I regret now not having gone and done the home visit and had a cup of coffee with her!'

It was a unique experience for Dolores to have a birds' eye view of the lucky hound's new life via social media.

'She was obviously taking good care of him. She had dog walkers and a backyard,' she says. 'He looked pretty rugged when he came into the shelter. He was coming off the streets and was quite depressed, and that was evident in his body language and face. If you looked at Meghan's Instagram pictures there was a huge difference: he was smiling and cuddling with her. He was very happy.'

Indeed, one of those dog walkers also had nothing but praise for Meghan's doting dogparenting. Irish writer Sarah Blake Knox, who moonlighted as a dog walker while working in television in Toronto, told the *Irish Independent* newspaper that Meghan was 'open and down to earth, warm with a dry sense of humour. She was always extremely friendly when I arrived and would welcome me into the house.'

While many of the dog owners she worked for weren't much for conversation, Sarah told the newspaper that Meghan was always happy to chat. 'This stood out for me as the majority of owners wouldn't even say hello. Meghan was different; she was one of the few people to treat me like, well, a human being,' she said.

Meghan's Instagram posts also revealed that she had chosen a name for her new furry family member: Guy.

'His paperwork from the pound just said, *The little guy*,' she told *Best Health*. 'I tried [some names] but he wasn't responding to anything, so I said, "Little guy" and I think he was so used to people calling him it that he responded. I said, "Your name will now be Guy."'

It's not uncommon for Dolores to stay in touch with people who adopt dogs from A Dog's Dream. She is something of a round-the-clock support service for inexperienced dog owners.

'I'll sometimes think, *I'll have a day where I'll sit and relax,* and then the phone rings and someone will say, "My dog is lost," or, "My dog is sick – what do I do?"' she says. 'I have to talk to them and say, "Don't worry, it will pass." There's a lot of hand holding, but I encourage people to do it. I'd rather they call me than put the dog in a shelter.'

But she didn't hear from Meghan again after she adopted Guy, most likely because she was already an experienced dog owner with the means to pay for any additional support she may have needed.

And possibly also because Meghan was busy falling in love with a prince.

Rumours about Prince Harry and Meghan Markle had been swirling for months by the time the couple finally confirmed their relationship in November 2016. News that Harry had an American girlfriend sparked a global fever of interest in every aspect of the relationship, from how they met to when they would announce their engagement.

But when word of the surprising pairing reached Dolores, all she wanted to know was what would become of Guy the beagle.

'Guy was my first thought, because I knew she was going to be so busy travelling. I thought, *Oh boy*,' she says. 'But I couldn't imagine her not doing what was good for him. She really liked him a lot and was very close to him. It was very obvious that there was a strong bond.'

Dolores's confidence in Meghan was well founded. Soon after her engagement to Prince Harry was announced in November 2017, it was revealed that Meghan would be relocating to London – and Guy would be making the trip with her. Sadly, Bogart was deemed too old to safely make the trip, so he stayed behind with close friends.

Guy settled into Meghan and Harry's new home at Nottingham Cottage, in the grounds of Kensington Palace, and reportedly won a very high profile new admirer: the Queen.

In perhaps the most extraordinary 'rags to riches' moment of his colourful life, Guy was spotted next to Her Majesty in a chauffeur driven car en route to Windsor Castle the day before Prince Harry and Meghan's May 2018 wedding. He reportedly also attended the ceremony and snuck tidbits from the plates of A-list guests.

Guy hasn't been photographed since then, and the Duke and Duchess of Sussex have now relocated to Frogmore Cottage at Windsor. They have also adopted a black Labrador retriever.

'A reporter from CNN came to interview me and she had also been to London. She said, "Don't worry, Guy will have plenty of friends and plenty of people that will take care of him,"' says Dolores.

Nobody involved in saving Guy from the kill list in Kentucky is immune to the charm of his inspiring tale. Alison Preiss from Pet Valu, the pet shop chain that hosted the Milton adoption event, told *The Guardian* newspaper that what happened to Guy is 'a total fairytale. Here is this dog that was in a shelter, nobody wanted him, and through this wonderful adoption he's now living in a palace, running around with the royal family.'

But while Dolores thinks of Guy often and is frequently asked to talk about him, she says he is far from the only miracle mutt that has found a forever home thanks to A Dog's Dream. The rescue has found homes for more than 1600 beagles since its inception, and she certainly isn't resting on her laurels after her brush with royalty.

If anything, the real miracle for Dolores is that stories like Guy's help to shine a light on what truly special dogs beagles are. In fact, rescue organisations in the United Kingdom have reported a 'Guy effect', with a sharp increase in the number of enquiries about adopting beagles since the Kentucky rescue dog's story made headlines.

'His story was really miraculous and I love it, but I have better stories than that where beagles have gone into people's lives and totally changed them,' Dolores says. 'I have some being trained to work with people who have PTSD. These stories truly are more amazing and more important to me. I'm really happy to spread the word about rescue dogs and how wonderful they are.'

Because that's the truth of it, isn't it? Guy was just as special when he was abandoned in a Kentucky forest as he is now that he lives a stone's throw from a castle. He was always a miracle mutt.

All dogs are.

CHLOE

From sickly runt of the litter to motorbike-riding ambassadog

Ken Eaton has always had a thirst for adventure. From throwing in his civil service career at a time when landing a job for life was seen as a cornerstone of the fabled Australian Dream, to riding motorbikes while everyone else drove family cars, to raising his young family in a series of dusty mining towns, 'conventional' has never really been Ken's thing.

Fortunately for Ken, his wife, Sue, shared his slightly offbeat approach to life. As they raised their three daughters, the couple often spoke about the grand motorcycle adventure they would undertake once the kids had flown the coop.

'It was always, "When the kids grow up we're going to buy a nice big motorbike and explore the world on it,"' says Ken. 'That was our dream.'

Ken was already a fledgling biker when he first met Susan Bartholomeusz at Perth's Governor Stirling Senior High

School back in 1966. 'My dad had helped me buy a little Vespa scooter to ride to school and Sue used to ride on the back of it with me,' he says.

He was about seventeen and a couple of years ahead of Sue when they met, but that didn't stop the pair from falling head over heels in love.

'I met her at a high school dance and we were together from then on. I knew what Sue's name was because her surname was so long that on her home economics apron it stretched from one armpit to the other,' Ken laughs. 'She always said she married me because I had a short name.'

They married in 1969, when Ken was nineteen. Sue was seventeen and expecting their first child. 'We were very young and we didn't have any money. Sue was pregnant and in those days it was frowned upon, but we were soulmates and we made a life of it,' he says.

From the very beginning, dogs were a big part of Ken and Sue's life together. Ken hadn't had much experience with pets, but the Bartholomeusz clan were definitely dog lovers.

'I didn't grow up with dogs. We had a cat and I had a budgie when I was young, but my parents were not really animal friendly. It wasn't until I met Sue, and her family were dog people, that I really became a dog person,' he says. 'All our married life we had dogs, mostly Australian silky terriers.'

A succession of much-loved pets went along for the ride as the growing family moved around Western Australia over the years. Ken secured an engineering cadetship with the WA government soon after finishing school, but soon realised it wasn't what he wanted.

'The cadetship was for ten years and I was earning $80 a fortnight [about $960 in today's money]. In the fourth year the pay went to about $95 a fortnight [$1150 today],' he recalls.

When he was offered a job with a private engineering firm with a salary of $125 per week ($1500 today), he jumped at the chance. 'I had all these people saying, "What the hell are you doing? Fancy leaving the government – you were set for life!"'

Ken's new job involved working in WA's Pilbara region, so Sue and the couple's one-year-old daughter, Belinda, moved in with her parents in Goldsworthy, a mining town 100 kilometres east of Port Hedland. Ken spent six months working at various mines in the region, visiting Goldsworthy whenever he could.

He missed his wife and daughter desperately. 'In those days, FIFO (fly in–fly out) work meant twelve weeks on and a bus ticket for one week off. Luckily I was able to jump on a truck every two weeks and go up to Port Hedland.'

When being away from his family got to be too much, Ken took a permanent job in Goldsworthy. In 1972, with the help of a nurse, Ken delivered his and Sue's second daughter, Kylee, in an ambulance at Port Hedland airport after a frantic dash from Goldsworthy aboard a Royal Flying Doctor Service aircraft. Daughter number three, Heidi, arrived 230 kilometres further south at Karratha in 1978.

'We lived in a caravan for a bit, then a small flat, and then a little house. We travelled around the state a bit, came down to the south-west, then went back up north,' he says.

Along with the dogs, Ken's beloved Vespa had also made the trips up north and down south, but with family life becoming busier by the year, he eventually sold it in order to buy a more practical car.

By the time Belinda started high school, the Eatons were once again settled in Perth and Ken resigned himself to several years without a motorcycle. He started his own engineering business in 1990, while Sue worked for a community social welfare group that helped young people find jobs.

'She was a volunteer to start with – she used to go and help the kids learn typing. After about a year they needed someone to work there, which she did, and eventually she ran the place,' says Ken.

Around this time, the family brought home a Samoyed, Sammy – their first canine companion that wasn't a terrier. She was supposed to be Heidi's dog, but it didn't quite work out that way.

'We bought her for Heidi, who was fifteen, to have something to look after, and to teach her some responsibility,' Ken says. 'We all loved Sammy, but she really became my partner in crime.'

Life was pretty idyllic. Ken and Sue were in love and both enjoying their respective careers. The girls were thriving: all three grew up and moved out, and Belinda and Kylee both married. They all doted on the family pet. Sure, Ken's passion for motorbikes had been put on the back burner – but he was confident there would be plenty of time for that later on.

And then everything changed.

In 1999, when she was just forty-eight, Sue was diagnosed with breast cancer. The news was shocking, but Sue's prognosis was good.

'She had an operation and went through radiation. She got treated and it was all cured. We thought we were pretty lucky there: we were all right, nothing was going to affect us now,' says Ken.

But while she appeared to recover quickly from her cancer treatment, it wasn't long before Sue began to struggle at work.

The organisation she worked for had been taken over by the Catholic Church, which reorganised the staff. Sue's job changed significantly and she was frustrated to find herself feeling out of her depth in her new-look position.

'She was finding it quite difficult to manage, and I guess they thought she couldn't cope with what was going on. A year after her operation and treatment they suggested she take redundancy,' Ken says.

He viewed the change as a blessing in disguise. 'I said, "Great! You can come and work for me,"' he says. 'But when she started working for me, things started to go a bit awry. I suddenly realised that things weren't quite correct.'

Sue often seemed confused, and started to behave oddly. 'At work, I'd ask her to sort out the mail and she'd do it, but then I'd look at it and think, *What on earth has she done?* It was just frustrating things like that,' says Ken. 'She'd always been a person who really took pride in her personal appearance, but she started to hate getting her hair cut or styled and she wouldn't wear makeup.

'Then I'd realise she'd had the same underclothes on for three days. I had to be sneaky and make sure I picked up her clothing and got it into the wash.'

Naturally alarmed, Ken and Sue quickly sought professional help, but were frustrated by the response they received. 'We spent a while trying to tell the doctors there was something wrong. They were saying it was depression because she was no longer working where she used to with her friends, but it turned out to be much worse than that,' he says.

As part of her cancer treatment, Sue had been prescribed a drug designed to reduce the risk of recurrence. Ken recalled researching the medication and seeing dementia listed as a possible side effect.

'It started to eat away at me, but I'd talk to the doctors about [the potential link] and they'd say, "Don't be stupid," he says. "Fifteen years ago people didn't know a lot about dementia, not like we do now. The average GP had no idea how to treat a dementia patient. Most people we spoke to thought it was only for old people. Nobody thought young people could get it.'

That made the diagnosis, when it finally came, so much harder to accept. Sue, only fifty years old, had young-onset dementia.

Dementia is not one specific disease, but rather a collection of symptoms that are caused by disorders affecting the brain. According to Dementia Australia, dementia affects thinking, behaviour and the ability to perform everyday tasks. Early signs include progressive and frequent memory loss, confusion, personality changes, apathy and withdrawal, and loss of ability to perform everyday tasks. Brain function is affected enough to interfere with the person's normal social or working life.

Most people with dementia are older – it's more common after the age of sixty-five – but people in their forties, fifties and even younger have been diagnosed. There is currently no prevention or cure for most forms of dementia.

Sue's diagnosis was devastating and terrifying for the whole family. 'There wasn't – and still isn't – anything for young people with dementia. It freaked Sue out knowing that she might have to go into a nursing home with old people. She would say, "Are you going to put me in a home?"' says Ken. 'It was very hard for the kids, too. Suddenly they had a mum who was a silly old lady.'

Often, Sue wasn't aware or wouldn't remember that there was anything wrong, so she would become angry when she found herself struggling to recall words or perform everyday tasks.

At other times, she was all too aware of what lay ahead. She and Ken tried to be proactive – they went to workshops about living with early-onset dementia and found local support groups – but the reality of her prognosis proved to be too confronting for Sue.

'We went to these courses and they scared her because she could see all these old people with dementia, but she was young,' Ken says. 'As it got worse they'd say, "Go down to this [community] centre and they'll get Sue involved," but we went a couple of times and it was people who were eighty years old singing songs like "Roll Out the Barrel." We grew up with the Beatles!

'They'd say, "Leave Sue here with us," so I'd sit outside in the car and after five or ten minutes they'd call and ask me to collect her because she'd be so distressed.'

Somehow, says Ken, they 'muddled along.' His business premises were attached to the family home, so even when Sue couldn't work she would still come and sit with Ken during the day. But as time went by Sue started to become upset when unfamiliar people came to the office, and it became too difficult for her to spend her days beside him.

For Ken, however, the most difficult part of Sue's illness was watching her memories of him – of the wonderful life they had built together – slowly disappear.

'We went to bed one night and in the morning when we woke up I gave her a bit of a cuddle, and I could tell by her body language that something was wrong. She pulled away from me,' he says. 'After breakfast I said, "What's wrong? Why are you being silly?" and she said, "You shouldn't touch me like that, you're my carer."'

Ken got out the family photo albums and showed Sue the pictorial proof of more than thirty-five years of marriage, but after that day he could never be sure if the wife he adored would know who he was from one moment to the next.

'Sometimes I was the boyfriend, sometimes I was the carer. We'd go shopping sometimes and in the middle of the shop she'd become frightened of me and try to run away,' he says. 'Other times she'd get quite angry and start hitting me.'

As Sue's condition worsened, she would become more confused and restless in the late afternoon. The phenomenon is known as 'sundowning' or 'sunset syndrome'. Ken and Sue would take long walks together every afternoon to try to alleviate Sue's agitation.

It was during these long walks that Ken started to wonder if having a little dog to join them on their daily strolls might be a comfort to Sue. The family had been without a four-legged friend since Sammy passed away as a result of diabetes complications in 2001.

With everything else going on, Ken wanted a smaller, lower maintenance dog this time. 'After having a Samoyed for ten years and picking up all that hair – we sold the house a few years after Sammy died and there was still hair – I wanted a poodle!'

He ran the idea past his daughters, who were enthusiastically onboard. And so, in early 2004, they went together to look for a canine companion for Sue.

They were disappointed. None of the pet shops they visited had the kind of dog they were looking for. One, however, urged Ken to come back later in the week, when a litter of puppies was expected.

'We went back and there were three or four little dogs in this cage, jumping up. I said to Sue, "Look at these ones, they're nice," but she just looked straight through to the back,' he recalls.

Ken followed Sue's gaze to discover what had transfixed her and saw a tiny, sickly-looking toy poodle–Maltese puppy.

'There was this little runt of a thing and the others were jumping on it and pushing it out of the way. I walked around a bit more and found some cockapoos, but I could just see in Sue's eyes that she wasn't interested. She said, "I want that one."'

Ken was dubious, to put it mildly. The puppy was clearly a weakling, not putting up any sort of a fight as it was stomped on and bullied by its more robust littermates.

The runt is the smallest member of a group of animals, such as a litter of puppies. Smaller and weaker than its siblings, a runt will struggle to compete for food and may be rejected by its mother. Runts are also more likely to have genetic or other abnormalities. In the wild, a runt is much more likely to die in infancy. Even among domestic pets like puppies, where human intervention can help, a runt's size and weakness, along with a lack of parental care, means surviving and thriving is far from a certainty.

Looking at the dog that had captured Sue's heart, Ken thought it would be a miracle if it survived. Just a few weeks old, it looked to be as light as a feather, and about as hardy. He didn't want to risk bringing a pet home for Sue that wasn't going to make it. He was sure the loss would be too much for her to bear. His wife was every bit as fragile as the puppy appeared to be.

So he asked the shop assistant what the little poodle's chances were. 'I just said to the girl at the counter, "Will this dog live?"' he says.

She told Ken she thought it would, and so the skinny little weakling became the newest member of the Eaton family.

The poodle was a girl and they named her Chloe. Just as her instant connection with the dog in the pet shop had indicated, Sue was absolutely smitten with her new friend. And Chloe blossomed in the glow of Sue's love: her shaky start to life seemed to have had no lingering effects, though even when fully grown she remained about half the expected size of her breeds. She enjoyed roughhousing with Heidi's larger rescue dog, and Ken suspects this helped Chloe develop a more robust constitution.

'My daughters joked that Chloe didn't know how to walk for three or four years, because Sue just carried her everywhere,' Ken laughs. 'I think Chloe just made her feel that she had someone of her own, someone she could relate to.'

It was a bittersweet realisation, because the truth was Sue found it harder and harder to relate to people as her dementia worsened.

'People would talk to Sue and she really wouldn't understand. Someone would say, "How many children do you have?" and Sue would reply, "I've got five." But with little Chloe, she was just her passion that no one could take from her.'

But while she doted on Chloe, her love for her little miracle dog couldn't slow the ferocious charge of Sue's dementia. By early 2006, her condition was worsening rapidly.

'She really went downhill and it became very difficult. They tried different drugs to reduce the symptoms, but it got to the stage where they said, "There's really nothing we can do. Go home, and eventually you're going to have to put her in a nursing home,"' says Ken.

One night in the winter of 2007, Sue stayed up all night. She paced the house from dusk until dawn, agitated and scared. She was frightened of Ken and wouldn't let him come near her. Devastated, he was forced to accept that he could no longer care for Sue in their home.

Sue was admitted to hospital as a precursor to moving to a nursing home. Her relentless pacing worsened. 'She would just walk all the time – she walked about 20 kilometres a day. She wasn't eating. She'd get cramps,' Ken says.

He asked the nursing staff if he could bring Chloe in to visit Sue. He was sure that seeing her beloved little dog would help. They said she could visit the courtyard outside Sue's room, but when Ken and Chloe arrived and the nurses saw how tiny she was, they let her inside.

'They said, "We didn't realise she's smaller than the hospital cat!" After that, Chloe became my constant companion at the hospital each day. She would run off around the corridors, visiting each person, but she'd always come back to Sue,' he says.

As the days passed, Ken started to notice improvements in Sue. She had all but shut down in the hospital, but Chloe's daily visits seemed to bring her back somehow. It seemed like a miracle had once saved Chloe's life – could the same happen for Sue?

'Chloe would just sit with Sue and cuddle her. Sue did funny things – she dropped Chloe a few times – but Chloe always went back to her. She just loved her,' he says. 'Chloe just seems to bring joy. The nurses said the older people in the hospital would wait excitedly each day because they knew the little dog was coming.'

Sadly, Sue's turn for the better was short lived. In July, she fell and hit her head, probably due to a stroke.

'She forgot how to eat. The doctors said they could put in a feeding tube, but I knew that was not the sort of life Sue would want. She just faded away,' says Ken.

Sue passed away in hospital on 23 July 2007. She was only fifty-five years old.

'Sue didn't know me, but she knew Chloe right up until her final days. That was a real comfort. And Chloe was a comfort to me, of course, because I was living at home by myself,' he says.

When Sue died, Ken felt as though all the dreams they'd shared for their grand adventures in retirement died with her. But slowly, Ken and Chloe started to adjust to life without the woman they loved so much. Ken's daughters encouraged him to look forward and think about the future, with one quipping, 'Dad, you can either have a girlfriend or a motorbike.'

Then, in February 2008, another unimaginable tragedy struck. Ken's eldest daughter, Belinda – known to all as Bindi – died at the age of thirty-eight.

Even in the depths of grieving these immeasurable losses, Ken knew he couldn't give up on his own life. The thirst for adventure that had fuelled his and Sue's richly unconventional life together was still there. Indeed, Ken, who was still only fifty-seven when Sue died, felt an even stronger desire to get out into the world – to celebrate life in memory of Sue and Bindi, and in honour of his surviving daughters and himself.

There was only one thing for it.

'In March 2008 I went and bought a motorbike,' he says. 'I pulled up on this big black motorbike that I didn't really know how to ride anymore and my daughters just said, "What have you done?" I said, "You said I could have a girlfriend or a motorbike – this is a lot less trouble!"'

Which is not to say that there wasn't a special lady in Ken's life. He was about to hit the open road with Chloe riding pillion all the way.

There's a term that originated in hip-hop culture that has made its way into the mainstream vernacular in recent years: ride-or-die chick. The sobriquet refers to a woman who stands by her partner through thick and thin, no matter what adversity she may have to endure.

It is, clearly, most commonly used to refer to female humans, but plucky little Chloe is every bit a ride-or-die chick. Not only has she been by Ken's side through the heartbreaking losses of Sue and Belinda, these days she is quite literally riding by his side everywhere he goes – on the back of his motorcycle.

When he first reconnected with his love of riding, it didn't occur to him to take Chloe with him. Flying down the freeway strapped to a noisy motorbike just didn't seem like the kind of thing a two-kilo 'maltipoo' would enjoy. And besides, where would Ken even put her?

But when he joined the Ulysses Club – Australia's largest social club for motorcyclists aged over forty – and started riding along with their Sunday morning jaunts, Ken started to feel guilty about leaving Chloe at home.

'I thought she should ride with me, so I spoke to different people and looked around for different things that would let Chloe come along,' he explains.

Finally, in a toy shop, he found a child's play pram that was the perfect size for Chloe. He put his engineering skills to use to create a throne fit for a queen. 'I reinforced it a bit and strapped it on the back of the bike, then I put a teddy bear in it in a harness and went down the freeway as fast as I could, and the teddy bear didn't fly out.'

Chloe's first ride with Ken was the Ulysses Club's annual toy run in December 2008.

'I put Chloe in her harness and off we went. I worried the whole way that she had fallen out and was flying out behind on the freeway, but we got there and she jumped out and was running around,' he says.

After that, almost any time Ken was on the bike, Chloe was right there beside him. 'We rode around Perth quite a bit and went down to the country. My daughter, Heidi, moved to Derby in the Kimberley for a while and I said, "One week we'll come up and visit you." We did a weeklong ride up there – a few thousand kilometres. That was our first big long adventure,' says Ken.

Since then, the pair has travelled more than 200 000 kilometres all around Australia, from the major cities to some of the most remote parts of the country. Their adventuring hasn't been without mishaps – in 2017, Ken collided with a caravan at Halls Creek in the Kimberley and spent a night in hospital (with Chloe curled up next to him in the bed) with a broken wrist – but the sense of peace he feels when out on the open road is too precious for Ken to pass up.

'The last eleven years we've been on the bike. Any spare time we have we're either riding the bike or planning a trip. We've done the Oodnadatta Track and all of Tasmania. Chloe has flown to Brisbane and Adelaide, and caught the ferry across Bass Strait,' he says. 'Sometimes we ride with our friends, but most of the time it's just Chloe and me. It's my therapy.'

The sight of a tiny ball of white fluff strapped to the back of a motorcycle isn't a common one, and Ken and Chloe understandably attract attention everywhere they go.

'Every single fuel stop takes me about three quarters of an hour because everybody wants photos of her,' he laughs. 'Even on the weekends when we go and have coffee somewhere, I hop off the bike and everyone crowds around her.'

In 2016, Ken decided to channel that attention into educating people about dementia. He set up his own charity, I Ride with Chloe to Fight Dementia, and sells patches and badges on his travels to raise money for Alzheimer's WA.

'I thought we'd get a little charity going in Chloe's name. Raising awareness is the main thing: I want to give people a bit of insight into what it's like to go through this, and also give them a bit of light at the end of the tunnel,' Ken explains. 'I got some patches and badges made, because bikers seem to like those, and I've got Chloe's story in a little folder that I give to kids with some stickers.'

Ken and Chloe's journey – in both the literal and figurative sense – also inspired him to write poetry about his experiences, and in 2018 he self-published a book, *Who Are You? Reflections of a Dementia Survivor.*

'They are reflections on my early life and from the time Sue developed dementia to her passing. An explanation of each poem is written in Chloe's voice,' says Ken.

After losing Sue and Bindi, Ken also decided to enrol in university and complete his mechanical engineering degree. He graduated with honours in 2013, aged sixty-four.

'It was something Sue had always encouraged me to do over the years, but I had never found time,' he says. 'Chloe would often sneak into the lectures with me!'

Ken is seventy now and Chloe is about to celebrate her sixteenth birthday – not bad for a dog who once had every-thing stacked against her, and whose survival was far from guaranteed.

'Chloe is in exceptional health. She's got a bit of arthritis – like all old people! – but we walk every morning and every night. She "talks" to everyone she sees and she loves to roam and play and run around,' he says.

If Chloe's long life is a miracle in itself, equally miracu-lous is the impact this tiny 2.4-kilogram ball of fluff has had on those around her. Chloe helped to give Sue a sense of purpose, and peace, in her final years. She has been a source of joy for the Eaton family as they have grieved for Sue and Belinda. And now she is not only helping to educate others about dementia, she's also showing that life goes on, and can be wonderful even when all seems lost.

Not bad for the runt of the litter.

JAKE

From fire survivor to sworn firefighter and fire department mascot

When a dog's life is saved in the face of enormous odds, so often that survival comes down to a series of what ifs. What if the dog had turned left instead of right? What if he arrived one minute later or left one minute earlier? What if she was adopted by this family instead of that one?

Perhaps that is the true definition of a miracle: a bunch of seemingly insignificant choices that add up to an unexpected triumph. On a bright April day in 2015, two very big what ifs meant the difference between life and death for a pit bull named Jake.

What if Jake's neighbour wasn't a veteran firefighter? And what if he hadn't been at home that day?

Bill Lindler has service in his blood. The 45-year-old spent twelve years serving his country as a member of the United States Marine Corps, including six months based in Australia. Upon his honourable discharge from the Marines,

Bill signed up as a volunteer firefighter in a rural part of his hometown of Newberry, South Carolina.

'I always wanted to be a firefighter and it was just one of those things where, when I got out of the Marines, I thought, *Let's try to kick this up a notch by becoming a volunteer*,' he says.

More than a decade later, Bill moved two hours south-east to the historic coastal city of Charleston. That's when his volunteer role became his full-time job; Bill has been a paid firefighter in the Charleston area since 2006, joining the Hanahan Fire Department in March 2015.

'The biggest thing was getting adjusted to it being a job. This is what I do every third day, not just when I'm called,' says Bill, who works a rolling roster of twenty-four hours on, forty-eight hours off. 'The transition was quite easy given my military background, as far as how things operate around the fire service and what we're expected to do and not do.'

But while he took the transition from volunteer to staff member in his stride, some things are never easy even after twenty-seven years as a firefighter.

'At a bare minimum we're also trained as EMTs [emergency medical technicians] or paramedics, because fire departments run their own ambulances. One minute you could be fighting a fire and the next you could be doing CPR on someone's grandma,' he says.

'It's not a job for everyone. It's truly a calling, because it is hard. We have a saying in the fire service: I wish my mind could forget what my eyes have seen.'

For Bill, some of the most difficult jobs are those that involve pets. He's a lifelong animal lover with a particular soft spot for dogs.

'I've always had dogs. I grew up out in the country on a farm and we had a little bit of everything growing up, from full blooded Weimaraners to your local shelter mutt,' he says. 'Dogs have always been a big part of my life.'

As a teenager, Bill had a black Labrador called Spunky. She was always by his side, and her constant loving presence was a formative lesson in the power of the human–canine bond.

It can be hard for any firefighter who has ever loved an animal not to dwell on memories of loyal, protective dogs like Spunky when confronted with pet loss in a fire. Thankfully – and perhaps somewhat surprisingly – four-legged fire casualties aren't all that common.

'Animals can be like kids. With the smoke and fear and all, they run and hide,' Bill explains. 'But most of the time, believe it or not, animals – especially dogs and cats – are very smart and intuitive. If they can find a way out, they're getting out.'

If they can find a way out. It's a very big if; one of those crucial questions that can make all the difference.

On that fateful spring day there was no way out for Jake the pit bull.

Unless you count Bill.

Tuesday 21 April 2015 was a typical day off for Bill. He had just wrapped up a 24-hour shift and was looking forward to spending the next two days at home with his wife, April, their seventeen-year-old daughter, Adrianna, and the family's four-month-old Rottweiler puppy, Bella.

As was usual for a midweek 'weekend', he was busy ticking items off his 'around the house' to-do list. He was in the midst of cleaning his truck when, in the early afternoon, he was alarmed to detect the distinct smell of smoke in the air.

Peering across his suburban street, Bill saw flames flickering in his next-door neighbour's backyard shed.

'This type of outdoor storage building is all over the place here – people buy these premade wooden sheds and convert them into "man caves,"' he says.

Without hesitation, Bill ran across the street towards his screaming neighbour. Half expecting a minor blaze that would be extinguished with a garden hose, his heart sank when he realised what the distraught woman was saying.

'She was screaming and yelling, saying, "We have dogs in there!"'

Bill doesn't usually bring his firefighting gear home after a shift, but in an amazing stroke of luck he had it with him that day. He instructed his neighbour to call 911, while he raced home to suit up.

'I started putting on my gear and by the time I got back across the street I could hear sirens coming. We were lucky we're less than a mile from a fire station,' he says.

While he waited for the fire truck to arrive, Bill saw a female pit bull and several puppies flee from the burning shed. But his sense of relief was short lived. There was another puppy, just weeks old, trapped inside.

'I saw this puppy trying to get out, and about halfway through a part of the ceiling fell on him. It was on fire, he was yelping and it was getting very smoky. It was getting harder and harder to see him,' says Bill.

Finally, the terrified little dog managed to wriggle out from under the burning debris.

But instead of running into Bill's waiting arms, the puppy turned and scurried back into the blazing shed.

Instinct kicked in, says Bill. 'I was thinking, *I've got to save this dog*. I went around the corner to where I thought he was, and was literally trying to kick a hole in the side of the building. I was trying to pull some of the wood off with my bare hands, but I just couldn't do it.'

It felt like hours, but only a few desperate minutes had passed. A fire truck from the Goose Creek Rural Fire Department was onsite and Bill's brothers-in-arms raced towards the fire.

With the help of Goose Creek's Senior Captain, Calvin Benekin, Bill dragged the heavy hoseline from the firetruck and positioned himself by the door to the shed. Captain Benekin doused as much of the inferno as possible, allowing Bill to see clearly enough to direct him inside.

'I waited at the door and knocked down all the fire, and I was yelling to him where I thought the puppy might be,' Bill says. 'Finally he found him over in the corner where I'd been trying to kick through the side of the building, huddled behind a couch.'

Captain Benekin grabbed the dog and ferried him out to Bill. Once clear of the choking smoke, Bill realised two things: the puppy had serious burns, and he wasn't breathing.

Fortunately, firefighters are well trained to save animals

as well as humans, and fire trucks are equipped with special-ist equipment such as pet-sized oxygen masks.

There wasn't a second to lose. Bill began a puppy-friendly version of CPR: mouth-to-snout breaths and gentle chest com-pressions. He also asked the woman who lived at the property to bring wet towels to try to soothe the dog's charred skin.

'One of the other firefighters got me the pet oxygen mask from the truck. We got that on him and got the towel around him. I was just trying to rouse him,' he says. 'He started coming around and tried to stand up on his own a few times, but he fell down because he was still weak.'

By this time another truck from a neighbouring fire department had arrived. 'One of the guys said, "We have an emergency vet right behind our station," so I handed the puppy to them,' says Bill.

While Bill and the Goose Creek crew mopped up the fire scene, the ailing dog was rushed to safety under lights and sirens.

Almost as quickly as it had begun, the emergency was over. (It was later determined that an electrical fault had sparked the fire.) The remaining fire truck rolled out and Bill was left to resume his Tuesday pottering.

But something had shifted. Bill sensed it. He knew he wouldn't forget the dog he had spared from the flames.

A few days after the fire, Bill couldn't shake his worries about the fate of the pit bull puppy. So he went to his neigh-bours' house, the burnt-out shed still visible in their backyard, and asked the owner's adult children how the injured dog was doing.

The answer they gave was like a punch to the gut.

'The young man that was living there at the time told me that the puppy was deceased,' Bill recalls.

He couldn't believe it. Despite the pup's burns and breathing difficulties, Bill really thought there was a good chance he'd pull through after the lengths the firefighters had gone to in their bid to save him.

But there was a twist in the tale.

When the man went inside the house, his sister spoke up. 'She said, "The dog is not deceased – it's still alive, but we're just not going to pay the bill."'

Bill didn't know what to think. He was appalled by what the young woman seemed to be telling him. Surely the family didn't really intend to simply give up on their seriously injured dog?

He had to know more, so he got in touch with the vet treating the puppy at the Animal Medical Clinic of Goose Creek. 'I asked the vet if the family needed help paying for the treatment, but he said that wasn't it at all. They had given the owners the paperwork to set up a payment plan and explicitly told them, "Put down whatever you can afford and we'll work with you,"' Bill says.

'Five minutes later, when they looked out into the waiting room, the owners were gone and the paperwork was blank. I thought, *This is just crazy.*'

The clinic was legally required to send a letter giving the owners ten days to make arrangements to pay for treatment and reclaim the puppy. Predictably, the owners did neither.

That meant the puppy would become available for adoption – if he managed to survive his injuries. And he was by no means out of the woods.

The pit bull had suffered burns to around 75 per cent of his tiny body, including all four paws. The intensive treatment he had to endure would have been an ordeal for the most stoic adult, but the vet estimated the little guy was only three weeks old.

Bill was warned to prepare for the worst. The puppy's chance of survival was slim at best.

'He was under 24-hour care for eight weeks after the fire. He was having to get special baths twice a day where they were scrubbing off the dead skin, and antibiotics around the clock for infection,' he says. 'Two of the vet techs were rotating taking him home because he had to have medication every six hours. He was on morphine for two months for the pain.'

And yet he hung in there, his feisty spirit well and truly intact. Despite what must have been excruciating pain, the tenacious little puppy was always happy to see Bill whenever he visited – which was as often as he could. He felt deep down that the dog would pull through, and when he did, Bill was adamant he would not be going home with anybody but him.

With every passing day, the cost of the dog's treatment grew, but Bill wasn't discouraged. He hadn't tried to pull apart a burning building with his bare hands only to see the puppy wind up in a shelter – or worse – because of an unpaid bill.

'I just said, "You just tell me and my wife what the bill will be and we'll pay it – I want him,"' he says.

His dedication to the wounded dog touched the clinic staff. A couple of weeks after the fire, Bill arrived for a visit and was approached by the practice manager.

'The vet was doing surgery on another dog, but the manager came and saw me and said, "The doctor wanted me to let you know that, since you're the one that rescued the puppy from the fire, there's going to be no charge for you – we're going to cover all expenses,"' he says.

'I'm sure the bill would have been $10 000 or more. I said, "It's okay, I can pay it," and they said, "No, the doctor feels that as you were the one that saved him, and now you want to save him again, he definitely deserves to be with you." I started crying. It truly blew me away.'

All that was left for Bill to do was tell his wife that their pack was about to get a new member. April knew her dog-loving husband had plucked a puppy from a recent fire, but she wasn't aware just how deeply Bill had bonded with the dog.

'I hadn't even talked to April up to that point, but she came home and I said, "Hey, remember the little puppy I saved in the fire? Okay, well, he's ours now,"' he laughs.

Fortunately, April was immediately onboard. 'She didn't take any convincing, even though we'd just got Bella. She was pretty well receptive to it when I told her the whole story and what was going on,' says Bill.

'We never expected him to be the little rock star he is.'

The puppy officially joined the Lindler family in June, when he was just shy of three months old. He was healing well, but needed ongoing treatment including antibiotics to stave off infection and laser sessions to help repair his burned skin.

As well as managing his ongoing health needs, Bill had another important task to tackle. His new four-legged friend needed a name – and Bill knew just what it should be.

In the early twentieth century, firefighters in the New England area were affectionately known as 'Jakes'. While the origins of the nickname aren't officially known, the most popular theory is that it comes from a key that opened the street corner fire alarm boxes situated in most Boston neighbourhoods. Inside each box was a small telegraph tapper that firefighters could use to send messages back to headquarters. In the days before radio networks and 911, it was the only way firefighters were able to communicate with their superiors from the scene of a fire.

The keys used to open the boxes were shaped like the letter J, and they were commonly called J-keys. In time, firefighters themselves became known as Jakeys or Jakes, and the slang term is now used to refer to hardworking, cool-under-pressure firemen and women across the US.

To Bill, it was a perfect moniker for a dog that had not only miraculously survived horrific burns, but had proven to be one cool customer every day since.

And so the plucky pit bull became Jake.

'Firefighters have been called that for more than a hundred years,' he says. 'This little guy survived, we estimate, seven to eleven minutes that should have killed him. If anybody deserves to be a Jake, it's him.'

So he was a Jake by name – and he was about to become a professional Jake, too.

As the excitement of welcoming Jake to his new home gave way to everyday routine, Bill realised he had a problem. His new canine companion still needed medication every six hours. With April working, Adrianna at school and Bill pulling round-the-clock shifts every third day, there would be nobody at home to administer it.

Fortunately, he knew a group of people he suspected wouldn't mind keeping an eye on a heroic fire survivor.

'I couldn't just leave him at home, so I started taking him to work with me,' he says. 'He was riding on the fire trucks with us and he was always at the station. I even took him to a couple of schools for fire prevention talks.'

He became such a beloved member of the team, who were grateful to have Jake at the station to greet them when they returned from fire calls, that he soon had his own bed – though he preferred to nap on Bill's bunk. He also had his own badge, and April Lindler even turned one of Bill's old firefighting jackets into a special uniform just for Jake.

It wasn't just the members of the Hanahan FD that embraced Jake as an unofficial firefighter. The fire station is located next door to Hanahan's City Hall, and Jake turned heads there, too.

Within weeks of Jake beginning his role as department mascot, city administrators decided to seal the deal.

'A couple of the ladies at City Hall fell in love with Jake and one said, "Hey, how would you feel about making Jake an honorary firefighter?"' says Bill. 'I said, "I'm game for it!"'

On 8 December 2015, the brave pit bull who very nearly lost his life in a fire was sworn in as an honorary Hanahan FD firefighter and official mascot. In his Oath of Office he vowed to 'make kids smile with [his] charming personality' and 'help them to learn about fire safety and what to do in an emergency situation.'

He 'signed' the declaration with a paw print.

Soon after, the story of 'Jake the Fire Pibble' was picked up around the world when a fan shared it on the social news aggregation website Reddit. He made his way to animal content site The Dodo, whose videos boast two billion views every month.

A Facebook page that Bill set up so that his family and friends back in Columbia could keep tabs on Jake suddenly had 28 000 fans, and his Instagram following swelled from 339 to more than 24 000 in forty-eight hours (@jakethefirepibble).

'I occasionally still scratch my head like, *Wow, how did this happen?* It was kind of a shock, but at the same time I can kind of understand the interest,' Bill says. 'It's a very good story of the underdog beating the odds.'

While the public attention is at times overwhelming, Bill is grateful to have a platform to not only educate about fire safety, but to dispel some of the persistent myths around pit bulls as well.

'I used his Facebook page to promote the positive side of pit bulls. I actually hate that term – there is no such breed as a pit bull; it's just a generic term for a type of dog,' he explains. 'I wanted to promote a positive outlook on the bulldog breeds in general.'

Jake is now four years old, and aside from a patch of bald skin that requires sunscreen in the summertime, shows no signs of any lasting problems as a result of the injuries he sustained in the fire. His only health issue is a grass allergy, which is treated with medication because Jake steadfastly refuses to stop rolling around on the lawn.

His hardy constitution is no doubt in large part down to the gourmet diet he enjoys. He dines on ham and cheese omelettes for breakfast and a cooked casserole of minced meat and mixed vegetables in the evening.

'I'm hoping he's just going to have a normal, long, happy, loved doggy life,' Bill says. 'I joke around with some of the guys at work that one day I hope I can live the life that my wife and my kids and my dogs have!'

Bill doesn't know Jake's exact birthday, but celebrates it on 1 April – along with his and April's wedding anniversary – based on the vet's estimation of his age at the time of the fire. Jake and Bella each enjoy a birthday party every year complete with party hats, gifts and dog-friendly birthday cake.

'It's for family and friends, and several of the guys from the fire department will drop by,' Bill says. 'Jake doesn't wear his party hat so much anymore because he just tries to chew and eat them.'

He doesn't spend quite as much time at the fire station these days, because as he's grown older Jake has become particular about the company he keeps. It's hardly surprising he should feel anxious at times given the trauma he experienced at such a young age, and Bill is determined not to subject Jake to any unnecessary stress.

'For whatever reason he became very people selective and started getting a little snappy with some of the guys. I get it – it's kind of like us. We don't like everybody we meet, and dogs are the same way,' he explains.

'I'd love to have him there every day but I can't be selfish. Jake is my boy and I've got to make sure he's safe, first and foremost. If that means keeping him at home so he doesn't scratch or nip anybody, so be it.'

Sadly, Bill doesn't know what became of Jake's mother and siblings; the adult dog and the other puppies he saw escaping the blaze as he arrived on the scene vanished within days of the fire. Bill's neighbours also moved away not long after the fire. If the family realised the pit bull on Bill's property was the burned puppy they abandoned at the vet hospital, they never mentioned it to him.

Whether he ends up as a working dog or whiles away his days simply snoozing on the couch, one thing is clear: Jake's life would be vastly different if Bill Lindler hadn't been at home on that day in April 2015.

'Jake is my right-hand man. It's just the bond he and I have. I don't know what I would do without him, honestly,' Bill says. 'My wife jokes with me occasionally, "I don't know who saved who." I always tell her the same thing: I think it might have been a combination of both.'

MILLIE

From disabled racing reject to bionic dog

Let's get down to brass tacks: there is arguably no breed of dog in Australia whose existence is more precarious than a racing greyhound.

According to Animals Australia, around 20000 greyhound puppies are born in this country each year. All are bred in the hope of finding a runner fast enough to win a slice of the $4 billion gambled on greyhound racing annually.

But around 40 per cent of all puppies born into the greyhound racing industry will never race. Instead, they are killed, and often not humanely. According to the Special Commission of Inquiry into the Greyhound Racing Industry, between 50 and 70 per cent of the 97783 dogs bred in the last twelve years were killed after being deemed uncompetitive as racing dogs.

That's up to 68000 dogs killed just because they couldn't run fast enough.

Most don't even make it to their fifth birthday. While the average life expectancy of a pet greyhound is twelve years, for a racing dog it's just four-and-a-half years. Only 10 per cent of dogs born into the industry live out their natural lifespan.

The picture isn't much prettier for those dogs that *do* make it to the track. Based on industry figures, the RSPCA estimates that more than 750 dogs are injured every month on greyhound racing tracks in Australia. These injuries are often catastrophic – think serious bone fractures and muscle damage – and can lead to death on the track or require immediate euthanasia. Sometimes the injuries are survivable, but the dogs' trainers aren't willing to pay for the necessary veterinary treatment and choose euthanasia instead. Some greyhounds even die of cardiac arrest due to the physical intensity of racing.

Away from the track, greyhounds are often housed in small pens, crates or kennels, allowed out only to train or race.

And greyhounds aren't the only creatures that suffer as a result of the racing industry. Though it is illegal in Australia, the RSPCA says that up to 20 per cent of trainers engage in live baiting: using live animals such as piglets, possums, rabbits and kittens to train greyhounds to chase. Bait animals endure horrific pain, fear, injury and distress, and one way or another will eventually die.

In 2015, after a television exposé of cruel industry practices, then Premier Mike Baird announced a ban on greyhound racing in New South Wales that would have taken effect in July 2017. Despite huge community support for the ban, it was reversed in October 2016 and greyhounds continue to race. The sport was banned in the Australian Capital Territory in 2018, while investigations and government inquiries are ongoing in other states.

Given the industry's appalling reputation, it could be seen as extraordinary that any greyhound makes it out of racing alive. But life can be tough even for those dogs that survive the track.

Animals Australia says many rescued racing greyhounds have been underfed, possibly because they have been kept on a restricted diet to keep them at a lean racing weight.

Compassionate people all over Australia are working tirelessly to get greyhounds out of racing and into loving families, but it can be difficult to rehome unwanted dogs that have no idea what it means to be a cherished companion animal. Few racing greyhounds receive adequate socialisation with humans and other animals, making them more likely to develop fearfulness and antisocial behaviour.

The industry's Greyhound Adoption Program operates in most states, but only about six per cent of all pre-raced and retired greyhounds are rehomed. The tragic irony is that greyhounds make perfect pets: they are naturally gentle, sweet natured and don't need much exercise.

It's a grim outlook for sure, and that's just for the healthy dogs. Imagine, then, how bleak the future might be for a greyhound puppy with a disability that would prevent her from ever getting anywhere near a racetrack; a disability that would require expensive, never-tried-before veterinary surgery.

A dog like that wouldn't stand a chance. A dog like that would need a miracle.

Like most people outside the industry, Nora Anderson-Dieppe had never given much thought to what life is like for racing greyhounds.

A lifelong dog lover, greyhounds weren't ever on her radar when it came to thinking about potential pets.

Nora was born and raised in Hong Kong, and met her English husband, Ed, when they were both at university in England. When they moved to Australia in 2007, they decided the time was right to add some four-legged friends to their family.

The couple adopted Yuki, a Pomeranian–miniature fox terrier mix, and Akira, who is also probably a terrier but whose particular mix of breeds remains a mystery. Going from having no dogs to two in one fell swoop was quite a change, and Nora and Ed were content to be a family of four for the foreseeable future.

But a chance encounter in a Sydney park soon changed that.

'I met a greyhound while walking Yuki and Akira and thought, *Why is this dog covered in scars?*' Nora recalls.

Shocked by the sweet rescue dog's appearance, she went home and started researching. She read everything she could find online about greyhounds and the racing industry, and was appalled by what she learned.

'I knew they raced but I never thought beyond that. Once

I started researching I thought, *This makes sense – this industry is about profit, so of course this is what happens,*' she says. 'Why would they be treated well? How could they be, in such a fast-paced industry? I guess I felt really guilty for not knowing that greyhounds go through that.'

As well as guilt, Nora felt overwhelmingly dismayed by the injustice of it all. It was one thing to have to give up a pet due to unforeseen circumstances, she thought, but to bring thousands of dogs into the world knowing most would be killed was unconscionable.

'I just thought, *That's not fair.* To actually breed them while not caring about their future really upset me,' she says.

Her internet sleuthing also delivered a local rescue group, Greyhound Rescue. Nora immediately signed up as a volunteer.

She mostly handled administrative tasks for the organisation, such as responding to emails and managing social media pages, as well as fundraising activities like manning market stalls.

Before too long, however, Nora agreed to foster a greyhound in need of a temporary place to stay while waiting for a forever home. As often happens, one foster placement soon led to another. Nora would have liked to keep all of them, but Ed was the voice of reason.

That was until 21 April 2013. Nora received a message via social media from a woman she knew who had previously been involved in greyhound racing and now acted as a sort of go-between for the industry and rescue groups.

'She had left the industry, but had lots of contacts. People would get in touch with her saying, "We've got this dog or that dog" and she would spread the word and try to find homes for them,' Nora explains.

On that autumn Sunday, Nora's contact wanted to let her know about an eleven-week-old female puppy that was facing a very uncertain future due to a mysterious injury.

'She said, "Can you get down there, because there might be something wrong with her and I think they might put her down next week,"' she says.

Without knowing much more, Nora and Ed jumped in their car and drove to Campbelltown in Sydney's south-west.

The puppy was living with a woman who worked as a whelper, a person who assists with the birth of a litter and then raises the puppies. It is common in the greyhound racing industry for trainers to send their pregnant dogs to professional whelpers.

'A lot of trainers just don't have the capacity to look after the puppies, so they send them off to places like this,' says Nora. 'She keeps the mothers until they've given birth, then she keeps the young ones until they're about eighteen months old and go off to their trainers.'

The woman had on her large property a number of dogs that were pregnant or newly postpartum, as well as dozens of puppies. Visiting the facility was a tricky situation for Nora. She felt torn because she understood that the woman had a right to earn a living, but she was also repulsed by the sight of so many innocent dogs destined for short lives in a ruthless industry.

After surviving brushes with not one but three trains, escape artist Charlie Puccini has lost his outside privileges during stormy weather. *(Ann Paynter)*

Burns survivor Fergus's injuries shocked everyone who saw them, but his indomitable spirit always shone through. He now uses that resilient retriever smile to comfort patients in a hospital burns unit as a therapy dog. *(Victor and Anngel Benoun)*

Staff at the Animal SOS Sri Lanka sanctuary couldn't believe their eyes when a terribly injured Kalu arrived at their gates with a smile and a wagging tail. She loves her life on one leg. *(Animal SOS Sri Lanka)*

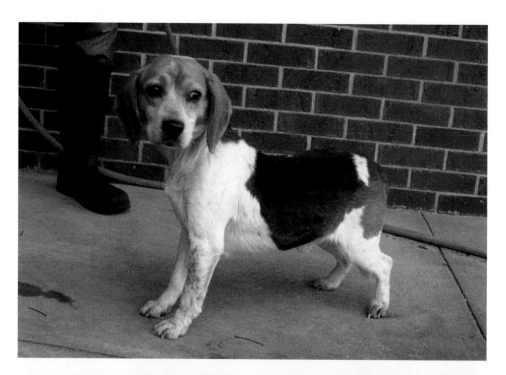

It's a true wags to riches tale: Guy was emaciated and depressed when he was found abandoned in the Kentucky woods, only to be adopted by television-star-turned-duchess Meghan Markle and whisked away to life in a palace. He even travelled with the Queen to Prince Harry and Meghan's 2018 wedding. *(Dolores Doherty; Noam Galai/Getty Images)*

She was the runt of the litter and not expected to survive, but Chloe became a source of immeasurable comfort to Sue Eaton in the final years of her life, and now raises awareness about dementia from the back of Ken Eaton's motorcycle. *(Ken Eaton/Verve Portraits)*

Jake the pit bull spends his days working hard as a sworn fire department mascot, but if firefighter Bill Lindler hadn't been at home the day his neighbours' garden shed caught fire it would have been a very different story. *(Bill Lindler)*

Originally named Lucky, Pedro was destined for the dinner table as part of Bali's dog meat trade before a good samaritan brought him to Bali Animal Welfare Association founder Janice Girardi. *(Janice Girardi/BAWA)*

When a mysterious injury cost greyhound puppy Millie her paw, her future looked bleak – until Nora Anderson-Dieppe and her husband, Ed, stepped in to help. Now Millie is Australia's first bionic dog, racing around on her 3D-printed foot. *(Ed Dieppe)*

He believed he could fly – but he was mistaken. What he can do, though, is run:
Daredevil is a three-legged force to be reckoned with on the dryland dog-sledding trail.

(Left: Primal Paws; right: Arctic Breed Rescue; below: Danni Monique/Flying Dog Photography; opposite: Ruthless Photos)

Roo was a courageous pit bull with so much love to give, but tragically cancer robbed him of the long life he deserved. His legacy lives on, however, through the Live Like Roo Foundation, which has helped countless dogs conquer their own cancer diagnoses.

(Sarah Lauch/Live Like Roo Foundation)

Surrendered to a rescue group by his original owner, Jax faced an uncertain future – until South Australia Police heard about his unique talents. Working alongside Senior Sergeant Tony Potter, Jax now has more than twenty 'collars' to his name. *(SAPOL media unit)*

Sammy vanished into the dense Queensland bush during a walk and didn't come back. Her distraught owner, Aubrey McCarthy, never stopped hoping for a miracle – and four years later she got one. *(Aubrey McCarthy)*

A culinary misadventure nearly cost Billy his life, but after a week at death's door he defied the odds and went on to become a national obedience champion. *(Frank Braes)*

A serious heart condition meant Molly wasn't expected to make it to three years old. With the love of her devoted owner, Sharon, plus a house full of foster pups to nurture, brave Molly recently celebrated her tenth birthday. *(Sharon Calder)*

'It was quite weird. I felt very hypocritical because I'm the type of person that doesn't like confrontation,' she says. 'It's her source of income and I get why she does it, but I also feel like if these people really did care they could at least try to make a change.'

Nora took heart in the fact that the woman had at least sought help for the puppy she was there to collect. From the scant information she had, she surmised the young dog's trainer no longer wanted her. If she was indeed injured there was no way she would make it to the racetrack, which meant Greyhound Rescue was her literal lifeline.

'I'd been told there might be something wrong with the puppy's foot, that she may have had an injury. When we got there the lady said, "She's missing a few toes,"' says Nora. 'She said the mother dog had bitten them off. She said, "Oh, she's fine, she just might not have those toes." It was very sketchy.'

When she finally met the puppy, Nora was surprised. The little brindle dog was full of energy and showed no signs of being bothered by what sounded like a very serious injury. Unfortunately Nora wasn't able to assess just *how* serious the injury was: the puppy's front left foot was heavily bandaged and she wasn't about to unwrap it.

'It had been bandaged up so we couldn't see it, but she was walking around on it, so it didn't seem like there was a big problem,' she says.

Besides, she and Ed didn't want to spend a moment longer at the whelping facility than they had to. Their goal was simply to get the puppy to safety as quickly as possible, so they scooped her up and left.

The couple took the puppy home to Willoughby on Sydney's North Shore and settled her in. Their usual vet clinic was closed, but they decided to make an appointment the following morning.

The little dog had a name already – Millie – and Nora and Ed didn't think there was much point in changing it. After all, she was a foster dog and her stay with them would likely be short. Her forever family could choose a new name for her when the time came.

According to the whelper, Millie had already been seen by a veterinarian who had worked in the racing industry and was renowned as a greyhound specialist. Nora thought it odd, however, that she apparently didn't require any ongoing treatment.

'She came with no medication or antibiotics – none of that. You'd think she would at least have been given some pain relief,' she says.

With the benefit of hindsight, Nora suspects Millie was in pain that first night. 'I think she must have been in a lot of pain because, having looked after a lot of greyhound puppies after her, in the beginning she was a bit placid and quiet,' she says.

'She would do this thing with her paw where she'd lift it up as if she'd stepped in something and was like, *Oh gross, what is that?*'

First thing Monday, Nora called Mosman Veterinary Hospital and explained Millie's situation. They told her to bring the brave pup straight in.

She and Ed met with vet Abbie Tipler, who was concerned when the couple relayed what they'd been told about Millie.

'When Abbie saw the bandages she said, "There's no way a good vet would wrap this and just leave it,"' says Nora. 'She undid the bandage in front of us because we'd been too scared of causing more damaged to do it ourselves. We thought, *We're not qualified*.'

None of them was prepared for what lay beneath the bandages.

They were met with a truly horrific sight. Far from 'just missing a couple of toes' (as though that wouldn't have been terrible enough), Millie was essentially missing her entire paw. There were no toe pads, just a raw, bloody stump.

Even worse, scar tissue had begun to form, indicating Millie's injury was several weeks old. She had likely been in agony for more than a month. The wound hadn't been properly cleaned either – it was a miracle she hadn't developed a lethal infection.

'I was just in shock when I saw this unfolding. Ed was mortified and started crying,' says Nora. 'He already had a really special bond with Millie. From the moment we picked her up they've had this really special connection.'

So little of Millie's foot remained that reconstruction wasn't possible – there just wasn't enough there to work with. The only other option, it seemed, was to amputate her front left leg.

'A dog without her paw is useless. She wasn't going to have any pads and her leg wouldn't be protected,' Nora explains.

The appointment duly made, a heavy-hearted Nora and

Ed took Millie home. Nora says Ed was particularly distraught at the prospect of his new foster dog losing her leg at such a young age.

'He said, "I just can't bear the thought of her leg coming off when she's so little – she's got ninety per cent of it left and she actually uses it,"' she says.

Ed had an idea. It was a little 'out there', but he is an architect and used to building things that might at first glance seem improbable. Fortunately, Abbie the vet also has a fondness for doing things that haven't been done before.

'Abbie is very progressive and is always interested in using the newest technology. She just thought there must be something we could do for Millie besides amputation,' says Nora.

When Ed and Abbie spoke again later that day, they discovered they were on the same page when it came to Millie's future.

She was about to become Australia's first bionic dog.

Dr Abbie Tipler loves a challenge. In her fifteen years as a general practice veterinarian, she has tackled her fair share of difficult surgical cases.

There was Mia, the Queensland dog whose throat was ripped open when she was kicked by a kangaroo. Abbie saved Mia's life with hours of emergency surgery and a blood transfusion from the family's second dog, Archie.

Then there was Snowball,* a Samoyed with a congenital

---

* Names have been changed.

bone abnormality called ectrodactyly or 'lobster claw deformity.' She assisted in reconstructing his affected paw in an Australian-first operation.

And let's not forget Rosie* the whippet, who was rushed to Mosman Vet after being attacked by another dog. Her airway was dangerously swollen and she was struggling to breathe.

Rosie would not have survived transfer to a specialist hospital, so Abbie had no choice but to perform an emergency tracheostomy while a specialist colleague guided her through the procedure over the phone. (Adding another layer of drama, electricians working near the clinic were threatening to cut the power, forcing Abbie to spend precious minutes persuading them to wait.) Rosie made a full recovery.

So when she was confronted with Millie the greyhound's mangled leg, Abbie was saddened but by no means discouraged.

'Millie had very little from the carpus [wrist] down. You can't just have a dog with a stump because they try to walk on it and it becomes traumatised,' Abbie explains. 'Amputation was the obvious option.'

But it wasn't the *only* option. As soon as she saw Millie, Abbie thought she might be a good candidate for a prosthesis – an artificial foot. It was the same thought that had occurred to Ed.

'Once you've amputated you can't put the leg back on, so the thought process was that we really had nothing to lose,' she says. 'Millie was a very young puppy and it seemed a real shame to amputate her leg.' She also knew that, being a young dog, they could train Millie to tolerate a prosthesis. 'She had the right temperament – if she had been aggressive or anxious it wouldn't have been right.'

Together, Nora, Ed and Abbie began to investigate potential suppliers of prosthetic limbs. They soon found a company in the United States, which produced a prosthetic foreleg and paw made from moulded plastic, rubber pads and foam inserts into which Millie's leg would fit snugly.

The limb cost $1200. Mosman Vet and Greyhound Rescue raised a combined $6000 to fund Millie's prosthesis and ongoing veterinary care.

But before Millie could test out her new leg, what remained of her existing foot had to heal enough to receive it – and that was easier said than done.

'Getting her into a condition where we could click on a prosthesis was a bit of a challenge because she had a big, open wound and didn't have skin covering it,' says Abbie. 'We tried to do a skin graft, but it didn't take.'

Eventually she had to remove more of the leg – amputating just below her elbow – and cover the stump with Millie's skin. The partial amputation went well, and by the time her prosthesis arrived from the US Millie had a neat, healed stump ready to slot into it.

Though she knew it was the best course of action, Abbie admits to feeling some trepidation.

'I hadn't done it before and I guess there were some nerves because a lot was invested, financially and emotionally,' she says. 'These sorts of cases are complex and there's a lot of different factors to consider. There's the owners' financial considerations, potential temperament considerations – a lot of thought has to go into getting the right treatment.'

There was a collective holding of breath on 20 August, the day Millie's prosthetic foreleg was clicked into position for the first time. But there needn't have been – the courageous canine, by then six months old, took to her new limb as if it had always been a part of her.

'I did think it would work. I just couldn't see why it wouldn't. We knew it would be a process and there might be teething problems, but I could see that it was going to work the moment we put it on,' says Abbie. 'I've worked with other dogs since where I'm not sure it's going to be as successful, but Millie just banged it on the ground and used it straightaway.'

Millie was the first dog in Australia to have a prosthesis due to a traumatic amputation and to have a prosthetic foreleg.

For Nora and Ed, it was an overwhelming moment. 'She took to it immediately. She got off the examination table and we were like, "Oh my god, she's using her paw!" It was amazing,' Nora recalls.

Dogs that sustain an injury to a paw or leg will often walk with the affected leg held off the ground, and it can be a habit that's hard to break even after the injury heals. Nora believes Mille adjusted so well to life with her prosthesis because she was already used to walking without it.

'Millie had been using her stump because we bandaged it to the max – she was walking on four legs with this huge boxing glove on her paw, so when we popped the prosthetic on it was instinct for her to put her leg down,' she says.

As a veterinarian, Abbie obviously loves animals – but she loves the science, the puzzle, just as much. But even for her, Millie's triumph was about more than just a pioneering surgery.

'It wasn't like any other case. It was new and different and quite exciting as well. There was a whole team of people who were involved, and we didn't want to let any of them down either,' she says. 'It's a cliché, but there was something a bit special about Millie. She was so cute, for a start, and so pleasant and so adaptable. She was so happy given what had happened to her. It was quite remarkable.'

That Millie had foster 'parents' as committed as Nora and Ed was also a key factor in Abbie's decision to try prosthesis for Millie. She wouldn't have considered such a time-consuming and untested process with caretakers who weren't prepared to do whatever it took for their dog.

'With prosthetics, you don't even want to go down that road with an owner that's not dedicated. It can be very expensive and there can be a lot of complications. When you have owners that aren't working with you it can make it very difficult,' Abbie explains. 'Nora and Ed were the best owners because they really worked with us. We're still in touch today, and that shows how closely we worked together.'

While Millie was undergoing her various surgeries and initial rehabilitation, Nora and Ed didn't talk much about what would happen to their foster dog once she was back on all four feet. But they knew they would eventually need to look for a permanent home for her.

'We decided we'd wait until she was desexed and then put her up for adoption,' she says. 'When that happened I said to Ed, "She can go up on the website now" and he said, "We can't let her go."'

Just like that, Millie had her forever family. The couple briefly tried changing her name to Miko, but she was well and truly Millie by then and the new name didn't stick.

The news that she would be staying with the Anderson-Dieppes wasn't much of a surprise to anyone who knew them.

'We'd take her into Mosman Vet for bandage changes every three or four days and they'd say, "Is Millie still a foster dog? Have you found her a home?" People were quite happy that we ended up keeping her,' says Nora. 'Everyone knew she was never going to leave!'

Equally thrilled were the 25 000-plus people who had been following Millie's progress and donated to her care via the Greyhound Rescue Facebook page.

'Because we were raising money for her, and to keep everyone updated with how she was going, we were posting pictures of me and Ed with her on her adventures,' she says. 'I think it was heartwarming for people to know that the life they'd been seeing was the life she was going to have.'

A life far, far removed from the greyhound racing industry. The life she deserved all along.

*

Fitting a prosthetic foreleg on a puppy is one thing, but adapting and changing the technology as that puppy grows up is another matter entirely.

After purchasing Millie's first two or three prosthetics from the same American company, Nora and Ed changed suppliers in 2014. They tried a company in Canada, but Millie outgrew her prosthetic while waiting for its replacement to arrive and got out of the habit of walking on her stump. It took intensive hydrotherapy to persuade her to use her leg again once she finally had her new prosthesis in place.

Determined not to repeat that situation in future, Ed and Nora took matters into their own hands, chalking up another first in the process: Millie is now believed to be the first dog in Australia to use a prosthetic created by 3D printing.

'We'd been saying, "We wish we could just 3D print them" and eventually Ed said, "Why don't we just do that?"' says Nora. 'We had the cast of her leg scanned and a 3D model drawn up, and now every time she needs a new one I literally just send it off to the 3D printer.'

Still a relatively new technology, 3D printing is much faster and vastly less expensive than traditional prosthesis manufacture. Millie is now six years old and fully grown, so her prosthetic leg only needs replacing when it wears out, which is usually every twelve to eighteen months.

'She really puts them to work. She loves using them in the water, running, digging,' says Nora. 'Whenever we see her using her leg we know we made the right decision.'

Millie doesn't wear her prosthesis all the time. Nora usually takes it off when the family is relaxing at home, and

Millie is quite adept at getting around on her three-and-a-bit legs.

Nora and Ed are resigned to the fact that they'll probably never know exactly how Millie's injury occurred, but it doesn't appear to have affected her in any way besides her leg. She may eventually develop arthritis, but regular hydrotherapy should help with that.

In every way, Millie the greyhound who once seemed doomed is queen of the castle.

'We call her Princess Millie because she's such a madam. If she's hungry she'll come up to the kitchen bench and just bark at us until we get her food,' Nora says. 'She sits on the couch and Ed sits on her dog bed.'

Nora's greyhound advocacy didn't stop with Millie. She has fostered several greyhounds since and started her own small rescue operation. She succeeded in having Millie's brother, Jack, returned to Australia from Macau's notorious Canidrome greyhound racetrack, which was shut down in 2018.

The only legal greyhound track in Asia, Canidrome was home to more than 600 mostly Australian-bred dogs. Industry body Greyhounds Australasia banned the export of dogs to Macau in 2014 after concerns were raised about the animals' welfare, but the government continued to issue export permits.

Greyhounds are sold and exported overseas for racing purposes to several countries, including China and Vietnam. According to Animals Australia, export not only places the dogs at risk of travel-related stress and injuries, it can also see them sent to countries without legal animal welfare protection or even result in them entering the dog meat trade.

Jack's story is just as miraculous as Millie's. He was the only puppy in Millie's litter to be sent overseas. Most of the dogs whose fates were up in the air after the Canidrome closure ultimately found homes around the world, but not Jack. Thanks to Nora, he came home in June 2019 and was adopted by a family in Queensland.

'Jack has really had nine lives. First he was going to be put down in Sydney – that's why he was sold to Macau. Then he could have easily died there,' she says. 'I campaigned to make sure he got a good home.'

It's incredible to think that Jack may have lost his life in Macau and Millie may not even have made it to three months old, much less become Australia's first bionic dog, if Nora hadn't had a chance meeting with a greyhound in a park all those years ago.

'I didn't want to be that person who says, "Can you please do something?"' says Nora of her decision to stand up for greyhounds in general, and Millie in particular. 'There was no reason for me to say no, so I decided I was going to say yes.'

Many happy endings are the product of chance – but many more happen because somebody refuses to accept the status quo.

As Gandhi once said, 'We need not wait to see what others do.' Don't wait. Act. Say yes.

DAREDEVIL

From five-storey fall to three-legged sled dog

Think of history's greatest – or most infamous – daredevils, and a handful of names spring immediately to mind.

Motorcycle stunt jumper Evel Knievel is arguably the best known of them all. From his first vault over a box of rattlesnakes and two mountain lions to narrowly escaping death in a failed jump across the 400-metre-wide Snake River Canyon in the US state of Idaho, Knievel is said to have broken thirty-seven bones during his long career.

Then there was illusionist Harry Houdini, who became wildly famous in the early twentieth century for sensational escape acts such as the 'Chinese water torture cell' trick and a stunt that saw him buried alive.

And let's not forget gutsy American schoolteacher Annie Edson Taylor who, on her sixty-third birthday in October 1901, became the first person to survive a trip over Niagara

Falls in a barrel. (She spent the rest of her life begging others not to attempt it.)

In more recent years, Alain Robert – better known as the French Spider-man – has made many hearts race with his perilous climbs up the sides of more than eighty-five of the world's tallest structures and skyscrapers, including the Eiffel Tower, the Sydney Opera House, and Dubai's 828-metre-high Burj Khalifa building.

It all sounds very impressive, but the thing to remember about these thrillseekers is that they were prepared for their daring feats. They did things that were definitely dangerous and probably foolhardy, but they had trained and practiced, and had a reasonable appreciation of the risks involved.

The same cannot be said for one member of the Maclean family's pack of headstrong Siberian huskies. This is a dog whose name reflects his nature with uncanny accuracy.

He's called Daredevil – and it's a name he well and truly earned.

But Daredevil wasn't his original name. Back in the winter of 2015, when he was bought by a group of international university students living in Sydney's eastern suburbs, the handsome red-and-white puppy was known as Oscar.

The students lived in a high-rise apartment. Perhaps they were inexperienced dog owners, or maybe they hadn't done their research, because it's fair to say they were unprepared to meet the needs of an exuberant twelve-week-old husky puppy. One day in July they went out and left Oscar locked outside on the balcony.

He didn't stay there long.

Huskies are working dogs with a fierce independent streak. They were originally bred by eastern Siberia's Chukchi people, who were hunter-gatherers and relied heavily on the dogs to help them find food during the harsh winter. In the summer their canine compatriots would be turned loose to do as they pleased until the snow returned.

Some time after Oscar's owners left him on the balcony, a tradesman working on a neighbouring building looked up and noticed the puppy perched precariously on a fifth-floor balcony.

'He saw him on the balcony and thought, *Is that puppy going to jump?*' says Anna Karas, NSW coordinator for Arctic Breed Rescue (ABR), the rescue group that eventually took Oscar in.

To the man's horror, Oscar did exactly that, launching himself over the balustrade and plummeting at least 15 metres to the ground below. Why did he do it? Nobody can say for sure, but it wasn't entirely unexpected given his breed's high prey drive and proficiency as escapologists. These dogs love people, especially children, but they can also be mischievous and are accomplished escape artists; they will dig under, chew through or jump over fences if the mood takes them. To say huskies are active, energetic and intelligent dogs is something of an understatement.

Whatever the catalyst for his death-defying flight, by rights Oscar shouldn't have survived a fall from that height – and yet, miraculously, that's exactly what he did.

The tradesman rushed the hapless husky to the nearby Kingsford Veterinary Hospital (KVH). He had a badly fractured leg, but incredibly, appeared to have sustained no other injuries.

Fortunately, Oscar had an up-to-date microchip and clinic staff were able to contact his owners. *Un*fortunately, the students couldn't or wouldn't make a decision about what should be done for him.

They hemmed and hawed for three weeks, neither agreeing to relinquish him nor giving the go-ahead for treatment that would give Oscar's broken leg the best possible chance of healing. There was a small window of opportunity to save the leg, and it was closing rapidly. All the vets caring for him could do while they waited was bandage him up, administer pain relief and keep him contained.

'Unfortunately vets are limited in what they can do. They can keep the dog comfortable, or if the dog is too far gone they can euthanise, but that's all they can do in accordance with the law,' says Anna. 'The students' delay was frustrating.'

Finally, the students made up their minds: they were unable or unwilling to pay for Oscar's treatment and instead surrendered him to the clinic. Immediately, the caring team at KVH scrambled to find a rescue group willing to assume responsibility for the little dog.

That's when Anna and ABR stepped in. When his treatment was complete, Oscar would spend several weeks convalescing with ABR foster carer Liz before being made available for adoption to a loving home.

In the meantime, Anna decided the courageous canine needed a new name. He was about to embark on a new life, after all – he deserved a name that reflected his tenacity and courage. She settled on Daredevil, or Dare for short.

'The second I saw him I thought, *There's no way Oscar is your name*. We named him Daredevil because he thought he could fly – he just forgot his cape,' she laughs.

'He was just confident from day dot. He was jumping onto tables, rearranging the pantry, chasing the fish in the fishpond. If he had four legs he'd be dangerous!'

Technically, Dare did have four legs – but he could only use three of them. While Daredevil's future now looked bright, the news about his leg wasn't as positive. The students' dithering had squandered too much precious time, and the window for saving his mangled limb was now firmly closed. Dare would need a miracle if he was ever to bear weight on the leg without pain, and he'd surely already used up his miracle quota when he survived his leap from the balcony.

He was still only four months old, and huskies can live to be fifteen or older. A lifetime of agony simply didn't bear thinking about. After carefully considering all the options, KVH and ABR agreed that amputating the leg was the best way forward. Life on three legs offered the greatest chance of health, happiness and, crucially, a home for Dare.

KVH vets performed the surgery free of charge. Dare then worked with a specialist rehabilitation vet, Dr Jaime Jackson from Primal Paws, to get used to his new life as a 'tripod'. Dr Jackson, who also worked pro bono, focused on strengthening Dare's remaining front wrist and ensuring he had 'rock solid' core muscles.

As well as his physical rehabilitation, ABR also worked with renowned trainer Glenn Cooke from Canine Evolution to help prepare Daredevil for life in his new home.

'Glenn assessed Dare and said, "Holy hell, you've got a real livewire on your hands!" The rehab was not a problem for Dare; it was just getting it through his thick skull that he had to listen,' says Anna.

'He was hard work, especially as a puppy. I'm really glad he didn't stay with the students because he was a headstrong boy and he needed the discipline. Most huskies are easy-going and dominate without you realising, but Dare made it very plain. He needed to learn his manners.'

In January 2016, it looked like Dare would get the happy ending he deserved when he was adopted by a Sydney family. Sadly, it wasn't to be. The family's circumstances changed and he came back to ABR about six months later.

'Everything we told them they needed to do to continue with Dare's rehabilitation, they were doing – for the first six months. Then life just became too hard for them. I went to see him and said, "He's not staying here,"' Anna says.

It was a blow, but Anna was not discouraged. She had no doubt there was a family out there that would be a perfect fit for Daredevil.

In fact, she knew just who that family might be.

Daredevil may be a superhero, but Geordi Maclean is something of a superwoman herself.

Geordi and her husband, Chris, have three children aged fifteen, ten, and eight. The couple balances the needs of their young family with demanding jobs in Sydney, and managing horses and cattle on their hobby farm at Mudgee in the NSW Central West. They also both compete in ultra-marathon events; in 2018, Chris conquered the 383-kilometre Moab 240 race in the US state of Utah.

And if that doesn't keep them busy enough, they also have six – yes, *six* – huskies with which the whole family competes in dog sledding.

It's a lifestyle busy enough to make many people want to take a nap, but Geordi and Chris are no strangers to either hard work or active dogs. Both grew up in the country – Chris near Oberon on the fringe of the NSW Blue Mountains, and Geordi at Goondiwindi on the Queensland–NSW border – where capable working dogs are worth their weight in gold.

'My dad grew sheep for fine merino wool and we had anywhere from five to eight dogs at any point in time. They were all kelpies and they went wherever we went,' says Geordi. 'They were working dogs, but of course we loved them as well.'

When she and Chris married and moved to the inner Sydney suburb of Redfern, they didn't think it was the right environment for a dog, though they really felt the absence of a canine companion.

Today, Redfern is a sought-after suburb among crea- tives, city professionals and young families (and its soaring property prices reflect its desirability), but when Geordi and

Chris first lived there it was notoriously dangerous and had a high crime rate.

In 2005, Geordi was mugged on the street while she was carrying her eldest child, then a baby, in a back carrier. When her mum fell ill and the couple were both offered jobs in Brisbane, it seemed like a good time to swap the gritty inner city for a safer suburban life.

'We moved up there so we could be closer to my mum, and while we were there I started running. Chris was already a runner and I picked it up,' she says.

Geordi would rise in the dark at 4.30 a.m. most days to complete a training run of up to 30 kilometres before work. Later, when the family started thinking about moving back to Redfern, she worried about her safety as a woman running alone at that hour of the morning.

'I was quite worried about getting out of Redfern on my runs. I knew once I was out I'd be okay, but I didn't want to go through that [mugging] experience again,' she says.

She started to think seriously about getting a dog to be her running companion. 'I thought I might get a dog, not necessarily to protect me, but just from the point of view that you're going to think twice about [attacking] a girl with a dog.'

At first Geordi thought she might get a kelpie, the breed she had so loved growing up. But while they're great sprinters, she wasn't sure a kelpie would have the stamina she needed in a running buddy.

'Kelpies are good in bursts, but then they'll go and lie under a tree,' she laughs. After further research, she decided a Siberian husky was the breed for her, and began contacting breed-specific rescue groups.

Sadly, arctic breeds such as huskies and Alaskan malamutes are among the dogs most commonly surrendered to rescues and shelters. All too often, people fall for the adorably fluffy puppies with the piercing blue eyes without properly researching or fully understanding their needs. Without plenty of exercise and mental stimulation, these breeds can become bored and destructive. They're also prolific shedders and their thick double coat requires more grooming and maintenance than many people anticipate. And they are vocal dogs, expressing themselves via a melodic howl that can be a bit much for sensitive ears.

Unfortunately, Geordi's initial enquiries didn't get her very far. She needed her prospective four-legged friend to be able to live with the family's two resident cats, Thunder and Wiggy, and the rescues she spoke to explained that cat-friendly huskies were rare.

'They said, "We maybe get one or two a year that we can put up with cats, but mostly we don't risk it because huskies have a very high prey drive and we just can't put a rescue dog in that situation,"' she recalls.

Geordi was disappointed, but undeterred. It wasn't long before she spotted a husky looking for a new home on the classified advertising website Gumtree. Her name was Dayna, and the moment Geordi met her she was in love.

'She was just lovely, very attached to me. She was so beautiful and ran with me everywhere,' she says. 'She was very, very timid and terrified of people wearing black, especially men – she would just go berserk and bark and bark and bark.'

The Macleans soon welcomed a second husky into the family. Roxy came from Arctic Breed Rescue and was supposed to be a temporary foster care case, but at the stately age of fourteen there was never really any doubt that she'd be staying for good.

The Macleans returned to Redfern in 2014 (where the quirky layout of the former pub they call home allows dogs and cats to have separate quarters). Tragically, a devastating incident claimed Dayna's life two years later. She was put to sleep after escaping from the Macleans' Mudgee property and killing several sheep belonging to a neighbour.

Her death anguished the entire family, especially Geordi.

'It broke my heart and I have never gotten over it. Roxy and I just wandered around the house for days, with Roxy howling and me crying,' she says. 'I made a promise to myself that I would never put another dog in that position. Now the dogs are tied up whenever we're at Mudgee.'

The long runs she loved became a sad chore for Geordi without her beloved Dayna by her side, so several weeks after her death Geordi decided to adopt another dog.

'Everywhere I ran I used to run with Dayna. I rang ABR again and said, "I need to get another dog and try to get my life back together,"' she recalls.

She was in luck: the rescue had a husky called Nala who needed a home. Geordi and Chris were only too happy to provide it. 'She is the most beautiful dog. She's so gentle and she's the queen of our pack.'

Not long after that, Geordi learned about dryland sled dog racing. Dog sledding on snow is an enormously popular winter sport in particularly frigid parts of the United States and Canada, but the Australian version sees dogs and mushers racing on dirt trails in forests aboard scooters, bikes or three-wheeled rigs.

She'd been looking for an activity that might suit her youngest child, who is on the autism spectrum, and wondered if sledding could be it.

'We'd been to an introductory day, but didn't really get involved with it at the time. Things were a little difficult with our youngest and I thought, *I need to get him out in the outdoors*,' says Geordi. 'I just felt like maybe I needed to get him out into the open air and try to get him to run around. I thought we'd try sledding for a season and if nothing else it would be nice to go camping in the forest as a family.'

The only issue was that, while she was sure young Nala would have no problem pulling a child on a scooter, she wasn't sure it would be much fun for sweet geriatric Roxy. She started to entertain the thought of adding a third husky to their growing brood.

As if the universe was eavesdropping on her thoughts, Geordi soon received a phone call from Anna at ABR.

'I'd been thinking, *Do I really want another dog?* It's a big undertaking, but when Anna rang and asked if I could take another foster dog, straightaway I said, "Yep, I was thinking about getting another dog anyway,"' she says.

The dog in question was a young boy with three legs who went by the name of Daredevil.

Anna approached Geordi to foster partly because she knew Dare had previously lived with cats and was a perfect gentleman with them, and partly because the Macleans were such an active family. Dare had become overweight and out of shape with his former adoptive family, and needed help getting back into top condition before he was adopted again.

'When Geordi took him into foster care he couldn't even walk around the block without virtually passing out. We didn't know how he would go with sledding because he was in such poor cardiovascular condition,' Anna says.

The Macleans certainly put Dare through his paces. 'Once he came to live with us we got him into better condition and got him strong and fit. In our opinion that's what's going to ensure he can live a long, happy life,' says Geordi. 'He's a big, big strong boy, and he's just gorgeous – just the happiest, friendliest, most beautiful dog.'

They also wasted no time in finding out if he was cut out for dryland sledding. 'I never doubted for a moment that he could handle sledding. We knew he'd be okay, but some of the sledding people were quite amazed. They said, "Wow, we've never seen a three-legged dog do this before!"'

But while he took to sledding like the proverbial duck to water, Dare's time with the family was only supposed to be temporary. He was a foster dog after all – soon he would go off to his forever home and Geordi figured she would adopt a four-legged husky to be a permanent member of the sledding team.

'The first year we did sledding with Dare I was saying, "He's a foster dog, he's not our dog!" The sledding guys just

laughed at me and said, "That dog's not going anywhere,"'
she says.

It was her eldest daughter, then aged thirteen, who finally
cemented Dare's status as a forever family member. 'When
the time came to start thinking about making Dare available for adoption, my daughter said, "Well, if he goes,
I go!" I rang the rescue like, "You're going to have to put
my daughter on the adoption list as well."'

But deep down, Geordi knew her teenager was right –
she couldn't imagine life without Daredevil. He had not
only proved his mettle as a sled dog, he was also swimming
and running regularly with both Geordi and Chris. He'd
built up to running 11 kilometres on occasion (though most
of his runs were shorter), which would be impressive even
for a dog with four legs.

'Huskies are nothing but trouble – they're so naughty
and they've got a mind of their own, but they're such interesting dogs. Ours are pretty well behaved because we run
them. They run five days out of seven and on weekends they
sleep,' says Geordi.

'Once we started doing all the stuff with Dare, and
realised how much he loved it, we went, "We can't put this
dog with someone who isn't going to do all of this."'

It was settled. Daredevil wasn't going anywhere.

There are dryland sled dog racing clubs in every Australian
state except the Northern Territory, and competitors regularly travel interstate to race. There are event classes for

very young children right up to adult teams. All dog breeds, and dogs of any age, can compete in sledding as long as they are in good health.

The Macleans compete for the NSW Siberian Express club from April to September. (Competition is weather dependent, as for the dogs' safety races aren't run when temperatures exceed 15°C.)

Now four, Dare's love of sledding continues to grow. Geordi competes with Dare and Nala in the shorter-distance events, as they're easier on Dare's remaining front leg. 'His front paw has to work double time and we don't want to put him in a position where he strains it,' she explains.

Of course, as far as Dare is concerned, missing a leg isn't the slightest hindrance.

'Dare certainly doesn't seem concerned about it at all. He just goes, *This is who I am*. He will pull the entire distance of the race. Nala will quite often go, *I don't think I feel like pulling anymore*, and just trot along beside him,' Geordi says.

'The focus and enjoyment and dedication on his face – and the worry that it might not be his turn to go out when the other dogs are going out – is just beautiful to see.'

In the two years since Dare moved in with the Macleans, their pack has also grown to include Cola, Diesel, Autumn and Isla. Roxy passed away in December 2017, while Nala is now five.

Energetic Cola, four, also came from ABR as a foster and has since become Geordi's most regular running buddy. 'Our boy Cola is the dog that I'm super close to. They had previously sent him out to someone who was breed experienced and he jumped from a standing position over an eight-foot fence,' she says.

Autumn, two, was purchased privately – she's the family's only non-rescue dog – while seven-year-old Diesel was a private rescue in 2018.

'Somebody was just getting rid of Diesel like, *Can anybody give this dog a good home?* A six-year-old husky going to somebody that doesn't know them is a recipe for disaster,' Geordi explains. 'He's a very handsome boy, but it's like he has ADHD and doesn't understand space boundaries. He just wants to give you kisses while sitting in your lap.'

Isla, meanwhile, arrived as a foster care case in October 2018. She was one of two husky puppies that had been surrendered to Alaskan Malamute Rehoming Aid Australia (AMRAA) at Mandalong on the NSW Central Coast. Geordi was told the pup's name was Dakota.

'I got a call from AMRAA saying, "One of these puppies has your name on it." I went back and said, "Look, I've already got five dogs!" but they were adamant I needed to foster her. They said, "She's really bolshie, she's got tons of attitude and she needs to be taught some manners,"' she says.

Once Geordi had relented and agreed to take in Dakota on a temporary basis, the rescue coordinator made a confession. The little dog's name wasn't actually Dakota, she said. It was Dayna – just like the beloved dog Geordi lost in 2016.

Obviously she immediately became a foster fail and stayed for good, christened with a new name, Isla. It felt like fate had brought her to the family, but Geordi is adamant there will be no more adoptions for the time being.

'Six is definitely enough,' she laughs. 'I didn't even want six in the first place!'

There's always a bit of civil unrest when a new dog joins Team Maclean. Things can get tense for a month or so while the huskies restructure their hierarchy, but if ever tempers fray it's usually Daredevil that plays the peacemaker.

'We really notice changes in behaviour when we bring another dog into the pack. It takes a while for everything to settle back down while everyone gets confident in their position. That's just how they work – they need to be allowed to sort that out and we just have to deal with it,' says Geordi.

'Dare and Diesel sometimes have a competition for who's higher in the pecking order, but if Dare feels like it's getting a bit much for anyone he'll step in like, *No, that's enough now*. He's a really gentle, kind boy.'

It makes sense that a death-defying dog named Daredevil would be the glue that holds his pack together. He has firsthand experience of being cast out of not one but two families that were supposed to love and protect him. Dare no doubt appreciates more than most what it's like to be cherished in spite of so-called flaws; to be celebrated for his perfect imperfection.

Dare has wisdom that even most humans lack. He knows the value of loving fiercely and being loved in return. He understands what a miracle it is simply to belong.

PEDRO

From being destined for the dog meat trade to a long life of love

It is a truth universally acknowledged that a dog that has met with misfortune and survived shall be given the name 'Lucky'. Not *every* hapless hound, obviously, but it's a pretty safe bet that most people have met at least one three-legged, one-eyed, scarred or tailless dog called Lucky in their time. It is the evergreen Dad Joke of dog naming convention.

It's meant to be ironic: they're given the name because they are supposedly the opposite of lucky. But dogs that have met with calamity and lived to bark another day are not unlucky.

Sure, there may be an element of rotten luck in getting lost, sick or injured, but these dogs made it through. They conquered adversity. They triumphed. They are lucky in the truest sense of the word. They deserve the name, because they earned it.

It's fair to say that dogs that overcome enormous odds to survive in a place not necessarily known for kindness to animals are the luckiest ones of all. They should perhaps be named 'Miracle' rather than Lucky (though admittedly that is more cumbersome to shout at the dog park).

Lucky the Balinese street dog could not have had a more fitting name bestowed upon him after he was spotted in the village of Pejeng in 2018. He was lucky not just because he was saved from an unthinkable fate, but because he was found by a friend of one of the Indonesian island's best-known champions of the underdog, Janice Girardi.

Janice, a 67-year-old American, has called Bali home for thirty-five years. She lives near the popular mountain town of Ubud with some thirty rescued dogs, most saved from appalling cruelty or plucked from the streets all over the island.

Animals have always held a special place in Janice's heart. Growing up in Pennsylvania and California in the United States, she was 'the kid who the dogs always followed home from school.'

'I wanted to keep them all, but my mother and I lived with my grandparents and I wasn't allowed,' Janice says. 'I first came to Bali in 1973, when it was paradise for both dogs and people, and started a little sterling silver jewellery company.'

It wasn't necessarily intended to be a permanent move, but then she met a dog that needed her help. His name was Honey, and she adopted him thirty-five years ago at Kintamani, a village on the western edge of the Mount Batur volcano caldera.

'I saw a man with this little puppy with white hair in the hot sun on a really tight rope. I was saying, "You need to give him water!" and I said I wanted to buy the puppy, but the man said it would cost US$100,' she recalls. 'I said, "No, that's too expensive" and the man said, "Well, we sell dogs' tails for one dollar."'

Janice persuaded the man to accept US$10 – a fortune in 1970s Bali – and bought the puppy. 'So then I had to move to Bali permanently because I had a dog,' she laughs.

As she became more entrenched in her adopted home, Janice became increasingly troubled by the treatment of animals in Bali, particularly dogs. There are hundreds of thousands of stray dogs on the island, most of which are starving and suffering from potentially deadly diseases including parvovirus, distemper and rabies.

In the 1970s there were no animal welfare organisations or rescue groups operating in Bali, and very few veterinarians, but Janice felt compelled to act.

'I would often see dogs suffering on the side of the road, and like most people I would always think someone else was going to do something,' she says. 'But then the dogs would still be there on my drive home, so I got more involved.'

She became a sort of ad hoc animal ambulance, ferrying sick and injured dogs and cats to the nearest vet hospital, a ninety-minute drive away in Bali's largest city, Denpasar.

She did this for years, until in 2006 she was presented with an opportunity to make her work a little more official. Janice befriended Paula Hodgson, the Australian founder of the Bali Street Dogs Fund (BSDF), which aims to empower Balinese people to better care for animals. BSDF doesn't operate its own animal shelters, but instead raises money for community outreach and education, sterilisation (neutering and spaying) programs, and access to veterinary care.

'Paula offered to raise money for me to run my own sterilisation van. She funded me and I got the van, then I got a vet in Denpasar to give me a veterinary team and we started going out every morning and spaying and neutering dogs on the east side of the island,' says Janice.

The mobile clinic was enormously successful – so much so that demand increased to the point where the vet was unable to keep up and suggested Janice take over. She was reluctant – her jewellery business had already been sidelined by her growing commitment to Bali's animal welfare issues – but ultimately she simply couldn't say no.

And so in 2007 Janice took the next step and founded the Bali Animal Welfare Association (BAWA). She partnered with BSDF, which continues to fund the desexing program and also partly pays for BAWA's schools-based education program and 24-hour emergency vehicle.

'At first I said, "Oh no, I can't do that," but I ended up doing it because nobody else would,' she says. 'You know how it goes: I ended up doing everything.'

BAWA's mission is simple: to alleviate the suffering of animals by providing emergency response and rescue, food and medication, rehabilitation and adoption, as well as lots of advocacy and education in the wider community.

The charity is funded entirely by donations and, along

with its large Indonesian staff, relies on the support of volunteers. BAWA responds to alerts of any animal in distress, from snakes to dolphins, but the vast majority of its work is with dogs and cats.

'Sometimes we get sixty rescue calls per day, and at least half are from tourists, then probably 25 per cent from foreigners that live here and 25 per cent from Balinese or Indonesians,' says Janice.

The organisation cares for about 300 dogs at any given time, which are housed in seven separate shelters across the island, as well as in paid foster homes.

'The demand is so much greater than our resources, but we do what we can. Our vet bills are US$5000–$7000 a month. Often I make up the [funding] shortfall,' she says. 'We appeal for donations, but we never have enough. The problem is just so big and we can't bring them all in, but we can't leave them on the street.'

Unsurprisingly, Janice and the BAWA team have seen some horror stories – but they have seen just as many examples of hope and determination.

'Sometimes we have dogs with broken spines that are paralysed, or dogs with parvo or really severe distemper that's gone neurological,' says Janice. 'We take in these animals and even vets will say, "Put them to sleep." But often – not always – they make it through. Their will to live is amazing. It really is a miracle that they survive.'

Janice is especially passionate about saving the indigenous Bali dog, the genetically unique street dog that she says is scientifically significant. The breed is critically endangered thanks to interbreeding, indiscriminate killing and cruelty, and the island's barbarous dog meat trade.

'Pure Bali dogs could be one of the oldest indigenous dogs in the world. Importing dogs to Bali was banned until 2004, so Bali dogs were just left to breed on their own,' she says. 'They stayed pretty pure until other dog breeds hit the island. We're trying to raise awareness of why Bali dogs are special and important.'

The Indonesian government restricted the dog meat trade in 2018, but BAWA's own research suggests it still thrives in Bali. A seven-year study by the charity found at least eighty restaurants on the island serving dog meat.

The way dogs are obtained for the industry is nothing short of horrific: they are simply rounded up off the streets, tortured, terrorised and killed.

But it's not just Bali dogs that are preyed upon by dog meat traders. Purebred dogs are increasingly abandoned to life on the island's streets, where they too may be caught and slaughtered for meat.

Since importation of dogs was allowed in 2004, Bali has been flooded with 'fashionable' breeds that frequently wind up dumped.

'People don't know. They want what's special and unique, and that's Chihuahuas and Pomeranians. They literally put them in birdcages and hang them from trees because that's fashionable,' says Janice. 'People get these dogs and they have no idea what the cost is going to be when they start getting sick, so they get thrown away because it's cheaper to get a new dog.'

It is admittedly a bleak picture. Life for stray dogs in Bali is harsh, and often includes an unimaginably brutal end. What keeps Janice and the BAWA team pushing against this tide of cruelty and indifference are the bright spots; the good news stories; the dogs that make it against all the odds.

Which brings us back to Lucky.

For people whose job involves catching and killing stray dogs for supply to Bali restaurants, it's all about volume.

These dog meat traders are a strangely efficient group. They rarely go out to trap just one dog; instead they will round up as many as possible before transporting them to their final destination and slaughtering them en masse.

That's why it is not uncommon in the island's impoverished remote villages to see several terrified dogs lying together in the blazing sun on the side of the road, their legs and snouts tightly bound with rope, tape or nylon twine to prevent their escape. Sometimes they are lashed to trees instead, or even hung feet first from poles carried across the shoulders of the men who will take their lives.

'When I first moved to my area in the countryside I'd see these guys walking down the street with bamboo poles and on these poles were dogs hanging upside down,' says Janice. 'Traditionally they will bind their legs and throw them on the side of the road until they've got enough of them, and then they'll go and get transport.'

The dogs' deaths are not quick. They are routinely tortured, before being shot, strangled or poisoned with cyanide.

'There's a weird concept here that the longer the dog is tortured the more tasty the meat will be,' Janice explains. 'Some people also believe that eating black dogs cures asthma.'

BAWA rescuers are frequently alerted to groups of dogs that have been rounded up, destined for the dinner table, and will enter delicate negotiations to secure their freedom. As abhorrent as the practice may seem to tourists and foreigners in Bali, Janice is adamant that cultural change will come through education rather than condemnation.

'It's very difficult, but that's why we believe that educating children – as many as we can, as young as we can – is the only way we can change the mindset of the people here,' she says. 'It may take generations, but we're committed. Our education programs show children that dogs have needs and feelings, exactly the same as humans. It is doing good, and you have to focus on the good or you'll lose your mind.'

Her approach was endorsed by legendary primatologist Dame Jane Goodall when they met at a group dinner in Bali in 2014.

'I asked her how she deals with cruelty day in and day out, and how she changes the mindset of this many people who simply don't care, and she said, "What *do* they care about? It's their children and grandchildren, so go to them,"' she recalls. 'The children are the ones that will go home and say, "Papa, don't eat that dog."'

Sometimes, against all the odds, a determined dog will manage to escape its restraints and flee. One such dog was Cinta – named after the Indonesian word for love.

He was rescued from a dog meat trader about three years ago, literally seconds away from death.

An Australian couple living in Bali fostered Cinta. He was their only pet, because he didn't get along with other dogs. When they decided to return to Australia a year later, they knew his chances of finding a permanent home where he could be the only canine resident were slim.

So they decided to adopt him – a tricky process, as the export of dogs from Bali is banned. They had to take a circuitous route via other islands before Cinta made it safely Down Under.

'He would have been unadoptable in Bali, so they decided they would go to all the financial trouble and months of work to get him through quarantine and into Australia,' Janice says. 'He was moments away from being slaughtered and now he's this really happy, loved dog living the life.'

And then there's Lucky. Nobody is quite sure where he came from, but he was first spotted in a busy street in Pejeng, a village just east of Ubud, during the first week of October 2018.

Lucky was first seen in the evening near the family home of a local woman called Wayan, who works for Sonia Monfore, Janice's friend. Sonia is also an animal lover, and regularly feeds street dogs in the area.

He wasn't called Lucky then, of course. He was nameless, but his good fortune was obvious: he had escaped the dog meat trade. His front legs were tied together with plastic rope, the binding around his front right leg so tight it had sliced into the flesh of his paw. His left leg was also injured.

But he was alive.

He must have chewed his way to safety and dragged himself to Wayan's neighbourhood. He was weak and emaciated, with every rib clearly visible and numerous scars criss-crossing his body. Who knew how long he had been on the run from torture and death.

Familiar with her employer's love of animals, Wayan immediately sent Sonia a message alerting her to the ailing dog. It was already dark, so Sonia advised Wayan not to try to catch the dog that evening; they would search in the morning instead.

Search for him they did, but they had no luck – the injured dog seemed to have vanished into thin air, which was quite a feat in light of his poor condition and severely restricted mobility.

There was no sign of him again until nine o'clock on the morning of 21 October, when Wayan called Sonia to say the dog was back – and he was in her house! Perhaps he had sniffed out Wayan's own three dogs, because he was now cowering inside a room, absolutely terrified. The rope was still wound tightly around his foot and Wayan could see a deep, gruesome wound.

Sonia tried not to think about how much pain the poor animal must be in as she told Wayan to close the door to the room and make sure her dogs were safely secured elsewhere. She also asked Wayan to try to comfort the frightened dog as best she could without scaring him further – the last thing they wanted was for him to scarper a second time.

Then Sonia called BAWA, whose vets arrived in the emergency ambulance within thirty minutes. By that stage Wayan and her brother had managed to corral the dog and cut away the rest of the rope.

Only once they got close to the dog could they see the full horror of his injury. The rope had been tied so tightly and had cut so deeply that his paw was all but severed.

He looked to be an indigenous Bali dog mixed with another breed, says Janice. 'He looks half Bali dog and half purebred dog – maybe a labrador or terrier. His markings around his face and eyes are Bali dog, but his ears are not,' she explains.

As he was loaded into the ambulance, ready to be whisked to Central Vet in Denpasar, Sonia had to come up with a name to include with his paperwork. She chose Lucky. It seemed appropriate not only because he had escaped slaughter at the hands of dog meat traders, but because she and Wayan had looked everywhere for him to no avail – only to have him somehow know to seek refuge at the one house where he would be guaranteed to find help.

And that help wouldn't just be short term – thanks to BAWA, Lucky would be safe and well cared for his entire life.

Janice suspects Lucky had been caught and restrained in a nearby village where there is a large factory whose employees are mainly itinerant workers from the island of Timor, 1600 kilometres away. The dog meat trade is even more widespread in Timor than in Bali, she says.

'We think they captured Lucky, tied him up and went to get another one, and he just managed to escape. Often they can chew through the ropes,' she says. 'It's a great mystery how he dragged himself to Wayan's house, but Bali dogs are really smart. They're survivors.'

Janice tried to approach the owner of the factory to discuss the workers' suspected actions, but didn't get far – she was loath to push the point and risk the workers losing their jobs for fear they might seek retribution by hurting other dogs.

Once in the care of vets, it was determined that Lucky was only about six months old. It was heartbreaking to think that virtually the entirety of his short life had likely been spent in fear, uncertainty, hunger and pain.

Upon examination, it was discovered that the bindings were so tight that the vets were sure he would lose at least one foot, if not both. He was also found to be severely malnourished and in the grip of a high fever, probably caused by his wounds becoming infected.

It all seemed horrendously unfair. Lucky had gone to unfathomable lengths to save himself from the dog meat traders, and his will to live was undiminished in spite of his terrible injuries. And yet his life hung in the balance. He was desperately unwell, and even with BAWA and the vets doing everything in their power his survival was by no means guaranteed.

Lucky remained in the vet hospital for a month, teetering on the precipice of death. And then, just as miraculously as he had found his way to Wayan's house, he rallied.

His mangled paw was saved and the antibiotics being pumped into him to conquer the infection kicked in. Lucky grew less wan and more alert. He even wagged his tail.

The vets also noted that Lucky had a good appetite 'and seemed to be always hungry', which was hardly surprising given what he'd been through.

Soon, Lucky was well enough to leave the veterinary clinic. He went to live at BAWA's rehabilitation centre and then moved on to one of its adoption centres, where he was renamed Pedro. It wasn't that the name Lucky didn't suit him; he was undoubtedly an incredibly fortunate dog. Rather, it seemed fitting that he receive a new name to mark the start of his new life. (Besides, BAWA has at least three other Luckys at that shelter alone!)

'There are still very visible scars that might always be with Pedro, but it was really a miracle that his leg was not lost,' says Janice.

At the adoption centre, Pedro also caught the eye of a visiting American couple. Initially they hoped to adopt him and take him home to the United States, but upon realising just how difficult – if not impossible – it would be, they decided instead to dedicate their energy to publicising Pedro's story and finding him an amazing home in Bali.

Pedro isn't even two years old yet, and he hopefully has a long life ahead of him that will be spent as a loved and loving pet. But even if he doesn't find a family of his own,

Pedro will always be part of the BAWA family. He will spend his days playing, napping and eating nutritious food at the adoption centre for as long as it takes.

'Pedro got away from the traders and he's now a really happy, healthy dog. He's with about thirty or forty other dogs in the adoption centre,' Janice says. 'We have volunteers who come in and walk them so they can socialise. He's doing really well.'

Though he is still young, Pedro is bucking a trend by having made it even this far. Bali street dogs risk life and limb literally every day. If they're not dodging dog meat traders they're trying to avoid being run over, beaten or killed. They might contract a fatal disease or be massacred by the island's own government, which regularly culls dogs in a bid to eradicate rabies. (It is a plan that is unlikely to succeed, says Janice, in part because many of the dogs killed are vaccinated against rabies, meaning there is no opportunity to establish herd immunity, and also because dog meat traders continue 'driving the dogs to different parts of the island, spreading rabies to non-infected areas'.)

One way or another, these dogs do not tend to live long lives. That's what makes Pedro's tale all the more extraordinary. He came so close to death by human hand, but he survived.

For Janice, it's stories like Pedro's that help her find the strength to keep fighting against culturally ingrained cruelty and callous indifference. She holds onto the knowledge that, for every Bali street dog that doesn't make it, there are others that have been spared unimaginable suffering thanks to her work.

'I can get really angry at people for pure cruelty, but they don't grow up the way I did, with a mother that loved dogs,' she says. 'I'm fortunate that I grew up how I grew up and had opportunities others don't, and now I can share what I know.'

And what she knows – what Pedro and all the other dogs have taught her – is that you never know where the next miracle will come from.

But there will be one. There always is.

ROO

From shelter death row to beacon of hope for dogs with cancer

How do you measure a miracle? Is it something whose effects linger for days, for years . . . forever? Or is it an instant, a heartbeat, a split second – a wrinkle in time in which catastrophe is avoided or fortune assured?

When a dog survives against all odds, must he carry on living for years for his life to really 'count' as a miracle? Or is conquering those odds for even a moment miraculous enough?

Maybe a miracle is all of these things. Maybe it's none of them. Perhaps it is simply being surrounded by love when once it seemed lost, and making sure that love continues to flow for as long as possible.

If that's the case, Roo the pit bull has worked countless miracles.

That Roo should have crossed paths with Sarah Lauch feels like fate. Sarah has always had a soft spot for animals.

Growing up in a rural corner of the US state of Pennsylvania, the Lauch family home was a sanctuary for a motley crew of critters.

'We took in every stray animal that came by. My mum and dad never said no to any animal that ended up on our porch,' Sarah says with a laugh. 'A lot of them were injured. We had a cat that didn't have a tail because it had got caught in something. It showed up on our doorstep and Mum rushed it to the vet.'

Over the years, the family's menagerie included numerous dogs, cats, guinea pigs, rabbits, and even a pot-bellied pig that became Sarah's father's best buddy.

'He walked with my dad and didn't need a leash – he just knew who his person was. Pigs are so smart. You would not believe the personalities they have,' she says. 'Our pig ended up having a better house than any of the other animals we had. He had his own barn and an acre of land.'

She didn't realise it at the time, but her childhood sparked in Sarah a fierce commitment to less-fortunate animals: those that are abused, neglected or discarded by the humans who should have cared for them.

'Growing up like that, just having animals treated as literally part of the family – giving the ones that are dumped a second chance, because where else are they going to go? – it puts into your brain this innate thing: animals really ought to be treated like one of us.'

No doubt because she had seen firsthand what happens when people fail to honour a commitment to an animal, it was a number of years before Sarah felt ready to have a pet of her own.

After finishing college she started interning in television, working sixty hours a week for a meagre wage that wouldn't stretch to cover a dog walker. She was desperate for a dog, but knew her lifestyle wasn't pet friendly.

It was only after she moved to Chicago in 2004 to work as an executive producer for NBC Sports that everything fell into place. She met John Schippman, aka 'Schipp', the man she would go on to marry, and they dipped a collective toe into the world of rescue.

'On my walk to work from where I parked my car I would look in the window of The Anti-Cruelty Society adoption centre and see these dogs in cages,' says Sarah. 'I would go in every week and when I met Schipp and knew he was The One I was like, *I think now I can do this because I'm not on my own.*'

The couple adopted a husky mix called Ralph. 'We went in there literally on the way to work and Ralph was in the corner of his cage, just sitting quietly. All the other dogs were anxious, but he didn't spend a lot of time on the adoption floor because the staff loved him so much, so he was in the director's office most of the time,' she says.

Being the first time either Sarah or Schipp had rescued a dog, they were caught somewhat unawares by the process. 'We didn't know we had to take him right away, so we had to rush and buy a crate, rush him home and then rush to work,' says Sarah. 'We got home and he'd got out of the crate and was sitting on the bed. We were just dumb!'

Once Ralph became part of the gang, Sarah was 'off to the races' as far as rescue was concerned. She signed up as a volunteer for Chicago Animal Care and Control's (CACC) City shelter. It is an open access facility, meaning it will take in any animal, whether owner surrendered, confiscated or picked up as a stray.

The shelter can house up to 500 animals in separate pavilions, and it is almost always full. Between October and December 2018 alone, CACC took in 3684 animals, including 1915 dogs. More than 560 animals were euthanised or died in care, and nearly half of those were dogs.

Sarah worked with the dog transfer team, liaising between CACC and the many rescue groups that pull dogs from the shelter and place them in foster care while they await adoption. It was her job to evaluate the dogs that were City of Chicago property – either because they had been surrendered directly to the shelter or hadn't been claimed by their owners during the 'stray hold' window – and let the rescues know which dogs she felt were the best candidates for adoption.

It was often tremendously rewarding work, but could also be demoralising. Dogs deemed city property could be euthanised at any time, regardless of Sarah's assessment of their suitability for adoption.

'I was in charge of a whole pavilion and I knew those dogs like the back of my hand. There were days when a dog would be there one day and the next day it would not,' she says. 'Saying to a rescue group, "This dog is amazing and deserves rescue," and then finding the dog gone was really, really hard.'

Her role was also enormously time consuming, eating up her day off work.

'I would spend all day Friday there, then come home and post videos of all the dogs to the transfer team's Facebook page. If I'm posting thirty dogs, that's my entire Friday,' says Sarah. 'My husband was getting upset that I was spending my day off there from ten in the morning until ten at night.'

After a couple of years as a volunteer, Sarah eventually stepped away from the transfer team, but remained active in Chicago's rescue community. She and Schipp adopted another dog of their own, a beagle–basset hound mix called Zoey, and fostered dogs every now and then. Sarah always kept an eye out for dogs in need at CACC, too.

Her less-intensive approach to rescue worked well until 5 April 2015.

It was Easter Sunday, and the day Sarah met the dog that changed everything.

There is a kind of bittersweet poetry in the fact that Sarah found herself on the City shelter's notorious 'death row' on a day that celebrates a very famous resurrection.

Sarah visited the shelter with her friend and fellow dog lover, Kelly Michael, who was looking for a dog to foster.

'We were looking for a pit bull type dog because we knew they were the most frequently euthanised, along with Chihuahuas,' Sarah says. 'We went into one of the pavilions and saw this dog lying in his cage.'

In a building filled with the cacophony of dozens of barking dogs, this one stood out – because he didn't make a sound. 'He was calm and not jumping for attention like the other dogs, so we took him out.'

The information card on the dog's cage identified him as number E332. It said his name was Cisco, he was about five years old and he had been surrendered by his owner.

Sarah and Kelly took Cisco outside and encouraged him to relieve himself. When he did, it was immediately obvious that something was amiss.

'He had issues urinating. It took a good five minutes for him to go to the bathroom, so I knew something was wrong – whether it was a blockage or a urinary tract infection I didn't know,' Sarah says. 'We knew it was bad, but we were hoping having him neutered would fix it. Once he got done peeing he was so loveable. He just hugged us and kissed us.'

The shelter was in the grip of a dog flu outbreak, and it was clear that Cisco had the virus. 'We could tell he already had it – he was coughing and had mucus all over his mouth,' she says.

With his urination problem and his flu, Sarah knew Cisco was at risk of being lobbed in the too-hard basket; he was a prime candidate for euthanasia. She and Kelly wanted to help the ailing dog, but they weren't sure how to proceed. They couldn't bring him to either of their homes due to the risk of passing the flu to their own dogs. They reluctantly attempted to return Cisco to his cage while they tried to come up with a plan.

But Cisco wasn't having it. He clambered into Sarah's lap and put his head on her shoulder, refusing to go into the cage. It was, she says, 'the hug that literally broke my heart.'

Plan or not, Sarah knew they had to act.

'If a dog comes into the shelter as a stray they have to hold them for a period of time, but any owner surrender is at risk of euthanasia because they're already the property of the city,' she explains. 'Kelly and I decided to put a "rescue hold" on him without any real plan. We just didn't want him to be euthanised.'

The rescue hold meant Cisco was exempt from euthanasia for four days. That bought the women precious time to figure out a way to guarantee his permanent safety.

They needed to get the word out about Cisco – and fast. So they took to social media, appealing to their contacts in rescue across the city. Cisco's best chance of long-term survival, they figured, was an 'iso-foster' home: a veterinarian or person with no other pets who could care for the sick pooch in isolation while he recovered from the flu.

'With this strain of flu they tend to get more ill after they get out of the shelter, almost to the point of pneumonia,' says Sarah. 'It would be three to four weeks of recovery, and it's really the worst period of an animal's life.'

Sarah and Kelly knew that finding somebody willing to step up for a sick dog was a tall order, but it wasn't long before their Easter prayers were answered. A rescue called One Tail at a Time agreed to pull Cisco from the shelter.

A vet offered to iso-foster and a donor volunteered to cover the dog's expenses.

From staring down the barrel on death row, Cisco had been thrown a lifeline. That he would make it out of the shelter felt like a miracle.

Sarah and Kelly decided Cisco needed a new name to go with his new start. They called him Roosevelt, or Roo for short. 'I can't even remember why, we just loved the sound of Roosevelt,' she says.

Roo spent several weeks recuperating at the vet's onsite boarding facility, where he had his own cosy room with a comfy sofa to lounge on. Sarah and Kelly visited him often. Once he was over his flu, Roo stayed at the vet a little longer for a routine dental procedure.

'His teeth were all ground down. Most were at the point where they were almost at the nerve,' says Sarah. 'We assumed it was from either Roo trying to get out of a cage or surviving by eating rocks and sticks. We weren't sure exactly, but we knew he needed to have the dental.'

Sarah was in her car when the vet called with what she assumed would be confirmation that Roo's procedure had gone smoothly.

She was entirely unprepared for the news she received instead.

Sarah pulled her car to the side of the road, her head in her hands. She could scarcely believe what she was hearing.

While Roo was under anaesthetic for his dental work,

the vet noticed a large lump in his groin. Concerned, he performed a biopsy and sent a tissue sample off for testing. The subsequent diagnosis was devastating.

Roo had bone cancer. Tragically, the disease was so advanced that chemotherapy was unlikely to extend his life. The vet estimated the sweet, affectionate pit bull had between three and six months to live.

Suddenly, Roo's urination problems and his former owner's decision to surrender him to CACC made more sense to Sarah. Did his previous family realise how sick he was? Did they abandon him at the shelter knowing that, one way or another, he would soon die?

'It was shocking to think he'd just gone in for dental and then got this terminal diagnosis. We thought he was going to be adoptable and have the best life ever,' she says.

Before his diagnosis, Sarah and Kelly had been posting regular updates about Roo on their respective social media profiles in an effort to find a permanent home for him beyond One Tail at a Time.

Now there was no question of Roo living with anyone else. Instead, Sarah and Kelly agreed to co-foster him. He would spend his remaining time being doted on by them both.

They decided to draw up a bucket list for him in an effort to pack as much joy and adventure into the time he had left. It included things like hiking, eating ice cream, chicken nuggets and hamburgers, being photographed by a professional photographer, enjoying a river cruise, and attending a Chicago Wolves ice hockey game.

'People donated things to him, including a night at the five-star Waldorf Astoria Hotel. It's very fancy, so walking in with a twenty-seven kilogram pit bull definitely made people look at us,' says Sarah. 'We had somebody come in and give him a massage. It was a really special night for us.'

Roo had already garnered a sizeable following of people moved by his narrow escape from the City shelter. When news of his cancer and bucket list reached his fans, they asked Sarah and Kelly to create a dedicated social media profile just for Roo.

'We posted about him on our own pages and people wanted to see more of him. The story got bigger because of his diagnosis,' Sarah says. 'I was reluctant at first because I just wanted to enjoy him and not be hassled by people saying, "You should try this therapy or that medication."'

But she was eventually persuaded, and Roo's fanbase quickly grew. It wasn't long before Sarah noticed something remarkable was happening in the comments section.

People weren't just following Roo's account because he was a cute pit bull doing fun things. It wasn't that they pitied him either. They were *inspired* by him. His message of making the most of every single moment was really resonating with people.

'I'll never forget seeing one comment on Instagram from a lady called Judy. She wrote, "Live like Roo,"' says Sarah. 'I said to her, "Do you mind if we use this as a hashtag?" and she said, "I'd be honoured – it's just so perfect for what he's doing."'

On 8 September 2015, five months after his diagnosis, Roo let Sarah know he was ready to go. Kelly had been out of town, and it was as though he had waited for her to return.

'He was not himself. We could just tell. He was in so much pain. We got him all his favourite things. He didn't want to eat – for a little bit he would only eat soft serve ice cream,' Sarah says. 'For a while he ran around the room and kissed each of us.'

And then, together, Sarah and Kelly held Roo as he slipped away. It was, Sarah says, 'one of the toughest days of my life.'

Just as tough was breaking the news to Roo's supporters. 'It was hard to figure out how to tell people, because they had been following our every move,' she says. 'We'd been on a national TV show and a lot of people had become really attached to Roo. I waited a day or two to make a post, and then I just said I knew it was the end of the road.'

Messages of grief and support came flooding in. Many people told Sarah that following Roo's journey had helped them cope with their own dog's cancer diagnosis. She was heartened to know he'd had such an impact in such a short time. A dog who had been unwanted and abandoned had left behind a tangible legacy.

Sarah began to wonder if Roo could keep helping people even though he was gone.

By November, Sarah had the beginnings of a plan. She had been so moved by the donations that flooded in for Roo after his diagnosis that she wanted others in the same situation to feel as supported as she and Kelly had.

So she started assembling care packages for other dogs with cancer. Each one included a blanket, toys, dog treats, tennis balls and a McDonald's gift card (she figured it was a safe bet that most dogs would be as fond of nuggets and burgers as Roo was).

It was nothing 'official', or even especially organised, but doing something constructive in Roo's memory helped Sarah process her grief.

'I didn't even think of establishing anything official. I just wanted to help people in the same boat,' she says. 'I was using my own money. I don't even know how I was getting people's information.'

But people were certainly getting Sarah's information. As word spread about her thoughtful care packages, and she started to receive more and more requests from pet owners, she began to think about helping people even more.

Sarah wanted to be able to fund cancer treatment for pet owners who couldn't afford it – and for that she would need to set up a charity.

'I thought, *Okay, I can do this as a foundation*, and started to research. It took a few months and about US$2500 to make the foundation legit,' she says. 'I knew that it would be worth it if people could donate and we could pay medical bills for things like biopsies and amputations.'

The charity began operating in February 2016. When it came to choosing a name, there was only one option: Live Like Roo.

Almost four years on, the Live Like Roo Foundation is Sarah's second full-time job (she's also still an Emmy-winning sports producer at NBC). Since its inception, the organisation has helped more than 6000 families. Sarah and one other volunteer have personally packed and mailed 2800 care packages to animals with cancer; that's up to forty parcels every week. The charity has also raised and distributed US$500 000 in assistance to cancer-stricken pets in the US, Canada and Europe, including $350 000 in 2018 alone.

She has the support of a six-member, all-female board of directors, but most of the day-to-day management of the foundation falls to Sarah.

'It's insane,' she laughs. 'All the blankets in the care packages are handmade – we have blanket tying parties. As many times as I've wanted to go on Amazon and buy them, these handmade blankets go the furthest of anything we do. They mean so much to somebody going through such a tough patch.'

Sarah's ultimate goal for the Live Like Roo Foundation is to give away US$1 million in veterinary assistance in a single year. But no matter how large the foundation grows, she is adamant the care packages will remain a cornerstone of what the foundation does.

'They will never end and I've never said no to anybody. A few people haven't even been sure if their dog has cancer or not, but I still send them,' she says. 'As much as the package is for the dog, it's also the worst time in somebody's life, and for them to receive a gift at a time when life is awful really means a lot to them.

'They always tell us their dog knows the package is for them. The most messages and pictures we get are from people saying, "Thank you, you just made my day." That makes me feel amazing.'

Live Like Roo also runs regular fundraising events, and Sarah has even set up a new rescue service called the Hot Mess Express. It takes in shelter dogs that are elderly, have life-limiting health issues, or have been deemed 'unadoptable', and gives them new lives filled with love and hope.

She says she never loses sight of what a privilege it is to have people donate money in support of her efforts.

'Schipp and I would really like to go across the US and say thank you to people. So many people, without meeting me or knowing who I am, are donating to us,' says Sarah. 'To trust me to know what to do with the money and where it should go, it's unbelievable. People are so giving.'

As committed as she is, Sarah's workload is intense. At times she admits it can get on top of her. Her heart goes out to every dog the charity assists, but some affect her more than others.

One such dog was little Wonton – renamed Wally by her new family – who had cancer and was facing euthanasia in a shelter, just like Roo. For a while, Wally's outlook was positive.

'We paid for all her chemo treatment – it cost $5000 – and she was cured for a while, but then the cancer came back and she died within a few days,' says Sarah. 'To help that dog escape death twice and then lose her so quickly was tough on my heart. We know all these dogs, even when we haven't met them. We know their humans and we feel for them.'

As painful as those stories can be, Sarah never ceases to be amazed by how deeply they affect people. 'People just care so much about dogs they've never even met. At this time and in this world, it's really nice to see people coming together in that way,' she says.

And on the days when it all feels like too much, Sarah remembers Roo. He is always in the back of her mind, and his legacy continues to drive everything she does.

'Sometimes we get kind of lost in the day to day and I'll think, *I need to post a picture of Roo*, because we have so many new people following us on social media and they need to know who he was and why we exist,' she says. 'He is always with me so I never forget where this all came from.'

She believes Roo connected with so many people – both during his lifetime and since – because everything he went through is a reminder that, while life may be short and sometimes unfair, it is also breathtakingly beautiful.

'Roo's message is so important, whether you're an animal lover or not,' she says. 'Even for non-dog people, it's sometimes nice to just sit back and say, "Hey, chill out – I need to take some time for myself and live for the moment, live for today."'

In a world that compels us to be plugged in and switched on twenty-four hours a day, it is frustratingly easy to forget what matters. That is the miracle of Roo: his time with us was short, but he mattered – and matters still – to so many.

And thanks to one sweet pit bull, hundreds of other dogs will survive their cancer and live long, happy lives.

In a perfect world, Roo would have lived to be one hundred. But if we can't have that, we can at least have the gift of learning to live like Roo.

JAX

From rescue pup to crook-collaring police dog

In the most literal sense, Jax the German Shepherd was born to be a police dog. He has top-quality working dog blood-lines, and even had two police dogs as ancestors.

But instead of fulfilling his apparent destiny as the long paw of the law, Jax was abandoned by his owner before his first birthday. When Jacqui Hart met Jax in 2017, he was unwanted, untrained and facing an uncertain future.

Jacqui and her husband, Max, have always had a deep love of German Shepherds. Max was a breeder before he met Jacqui, and the Adelaide couple has rarely been without at least one pet German Shepherd in the years since.

In 2016 they were devastated when their brother-and-sister dogs, Nyssa and Bo, passed away in quick succession at the impressive age of fourteen. They dealt with their grief with the help of a new addition: a puppy called Grace.

'I threw myself into meeting other people with German Shepherds to try to get over the two we had lost,' Jacqui says.

One of the dog-loving kindred spirits she met was Michelle de Veau, who had previously owned a puppy from Max's kennel and volunteers for the German Shepherd Dog Rescue South Australia (GSDRSA) group.

Jacqui decided to join GSDRSA, whose mission is to rehabilitate and rehome dogs that have found themselves without a permanent home through no fault of their own. She spent a year volunteering as the group's adoption co-ordinator, processing adoption applications and arranging for other volunteers to carry out property inspections to ensure prospective adopters had a suitable home for a shepherd.

Though today they are a popular choice as family pets, German Shepherds were originally bred to work. Along with Belgian and Dutch Shepherds, the German Shepherd developed from the so-called 'continental shepherd dog' that was common in north-west Europe in the late nine-teenth century. They were mainly used to herd sheep and protect their flocks from predators.

The breed is still known for its above-average energy and fierce intelligence, and needs an owner that can meet its need for both physical and intellectual challenge. Unfortu-nately, people are sometimes naïve about their capacity to meet those needs and realise too late that they're not equipped to cope with their big, rambunctious dogs.

Jacqui's puppy, Grace, was only a few months old when, in September 2016, Michelle told Jacqui about a dog called Buddy who needed a foster home.

'She said, "You don't know anyone that could do a three-week foster for me, do you?" I didn't think she meant me, because we had a sixteen-week-old puppy, but she did mean me. She sucked me in,' Jacqui says with a laugh. 'We went and got Buddy and we didn't even get to the end of week two before I rang Michelle and said, "He just has to stay."'

GSDRSA doesn't have its own shelter, but operates through a network of foster carers like Jacqui. Dogs of any breed rarely cope well in noisy, chaotic shelters, so the goal of rescue groups is to get them into a calm, consistent foster home as quickly as possible.

'German Shepherds in particular have a really bad record in that kennel environment. Buddy was a case in point: he'd spent six months in the shelter. They had classified him as an aggressive, high risk, "dangerous" dog,' says Jacqui.

When he was finally released into foster care and came to Jacqui and Max, they realised immediately that he didn't deserve any of those labels; he was simply overwhelmed and stressed by his extended stay in the shelter.

'He did not have an aggressive bone in his body, but he did have a bad reaction to kennel life. He was just incredibly frustrated.'

It was unusual for the rescue to take in a younger dog like Buddy, says Jacqui. He was thought to be about six when he came into care, and most of GSDRSA's work is with much older shepherds.

'We've had older owners who have had to go into care; ill owners who couldn't walk their dogs anymore and felt it was kinder to relinquish them,' she says. 'It's usually people who have had a really good life with their dog, or have given it a good go and realised they've just underestimated the requirements of the animal and look for a better home.'

Some of the German Shepherds that come to the rescue are chronically ill with degenerative conditions such as arthritis and hip dysplasia, an inherited disease that commonly affects the breed. But even when they're elderly and sick, GSDRSA has a no-kill policy. They will do whatever it takes to find each dog a forever family.

'Your heart goes out to each one of them. We believe that each one of them deserves a home and a good life,' says Jacqui. 'There is a beautiful home for every dog, and we do have some beautiful outcomes.'

With senior dogs making up the bulk of their caseload, it was *really* unusual when GSDRA heard about a nine-month-old puppy whose owner wanted to surrender him in May 2017.

The dog's name was Floki and he was purchased from a reputable breeder by a young man who lived at home with his parents.

But the man apparently didn't realise his adorable new puppy came from a long line of working dogs. The little dog's energy levels and need for mental stimulation were off the charts compared to German Shepherds bred for show or pet homes.

When his new owner's work commitments began to take him away from home for longer and longer hours, Floki was largely left to his own devices.

'He was left in a suburban backyard with the lad's mum and dad, who were older and couldn't walk him or keep him from jumping at the fence,' Jacqui says. 'He approached the rescue and said, "I think I have to relinquish him."'

When GSDRSA agreed to take him in, it fell to Jacqui as adoption coordinator to find a temporary home for Floki. The moment she met him, she understood why his former owner had felt unable to manage.

'We just did not know what we'd got when we got him. He was a young boy in an adult body by then, and extremely athletic. He was just beginning to become really, really active,' she says. 'No wonder this lad couldn't cope with him – Floki just sucked up everything we threw at him.'

He was in perpetual motion – the German Shepherd equivalent of Winnie the Pooh's rambunctious Tigger. Jacqui wasn't sure even an experienced GSDRSA foster carer would be able to handle him.

Concerned about Floki's adoption prospects, Jacqui decided to call in reinforcements. She had him sent to Dennis and Sue Smith, then owners of the Windamere boarding kennel at Clarendon in the Adelaide Hills.

It might have been a kennel, but Windamere is a holiday resort compared to the austere shelters in which dogs so often struggle.

'Dennis and Sue often took our dogs if we didn't have a foster home for them, because they have lots of acres and the boarders are allowed out to run and play with the other dogs,' says Jacqui.

Plus, Dennis Smith is a retired police officer and accredited dog trainer. If anybody could help her assess Floki and figure out a plan for his future, Jacqui knew it was Dennis.

Floki was duly delivered to Windamere, and the first thing Dennis did was change his name. He christened him Lloyd after Sergeant Lloyd Morley, the first officer in charge of the South Australia Police (SAPOL) dog unit in the 1970s.

The first time Jacqui visited Windamere to meet Lloyd in person, her fears about his suitability as a pet were confirmed.

'Sue rang me up and said, "Jacqui, can you come out and see what you think of this dog?" I got there and I could see his head bobbing up and down behind a ten-foot fence. I could hear him, too,' she says.

'He came up to the fence and he was so frenzied that I thought, *Oh my goodness, I couldn't recommend that any of our potential adopters come and meet you.* He was clearly a real working dog and I knew I was going to have to go home and have a good think about what to do for him.'

But Dennis's links to SAPOL and choice of name for Lloyd sparked a memory in Jacqui. She recalled that a former neighbour of hers had a son-in-law who was involved with the police dog unit.

She had an idea.

'We always say you wouldn't want one of our dogs as a pet dog. They'll landscape your garden for you!'

So says Senior Constable First Class Simon Rosenhahn, a SAPOL police dog handler. His primary role with the police is to train and work his own dog, Ben, but he also serves as the officer in charge of police dog 'recruitment'.

Simon knows precisely which qualities to look for in a future police K9 – and it's essentially the opposite of what most dog owners would want in a pet.

'With German Shepherds in particular, there's a big difference between a show line and a working line. To find a suitable dog for police work is pretty hard,' he explains. 'We want a dog with a high prey drive that will stand up for himself. He needs to be aware of his surroundings and show natural suspicion – but the next minute we could be doing a talk at a kindy, so the dog has also got to have a stable temperament and rock solid nerves.'

The police dog unit in South Australia is more than forty years old, but it's only in the past five years that SAPOL has implemented set procedures for acquiring dogs.

Some eastern states police forces have up to sixty dogs, but SAPOL has just twelve general purpose police dogs – all German Shepherds – as well as twelve Labrador retrievers that work as detection dogs. There was never any real need for access to a constant stream of fresh canine talent. Nor is there the budget that some larger units have: puppies from leading working dog breeders cost thousands of dollars, and the cost of training a police dog can run into the tens of thousands.

'We're quite a small unit, so we'd never really explored the option of having our own breeding program. Most of our dogs would be donated or we'd advertise in the newspapers asking if anybody had a suitable dog,' says Simon.

'Maybe ten or fifteen years ago we dabbled in getting some local breeders onside, but it was very haphazard and there wasn't any real structure to it.'

But while the ad hoc approach to police dog recruitment had worked relatively well over the years, the lack of succession planning sometimes left SAPOL scrambling.

'We've had dogs supplied to us from Queensland Police, New South Wales, New Zealand. There were no plans in place for having dogs coming up through the ranks to replace dogs that were going to retire,' Simon says. 'It was always a case of phoning up madly: "Do you have any dogs?"'

When Simon's own dog, Koda, was stabbed in the chest and critically injured while on duty in 2013, he knew it was time to get a bit more organised.

'Koda was offline while he recovered. I got another dog, but it didn't work out, so I found myself without a dog,' he says. (Koda made a full recovery and returned to duty in 2014, passing away in 2018 aged eleven.) 'I got in touch with Victoria Police and they put me in touch with the breeder they were using. That led to us getting more of our dogs through breeders.'

At the same time, Simon and SAPOL were still committed to assessing the potential of any dog that came up through other avenues. 'We've always said that if a dog comes up another way we'll have a look at them. If a dog comes out of the blue we'd be fools not to at least have a look.'

That's what happened on 24 June 2017, when Jacqui Hart got in touch. Jacqui is friends with Simon's mother-in-law – his wife's family and the Harts were once neighbours and have remained close friends.

'I've known Jacqui for more than twenty-five years. She had spoken to my mother-in-law, who passed on my contact details, and Jacqui let me know about Lloyd,' he says.

Jacqui sent Simon a copy of Lloyd's pedigree papers, which showed his lineage. Simon just about fell off his chair when he saw where Lloyd had come from.

'He's got some lines from one of breeders that we use. There are two police dogs going back a couple of generations in his breeding, so I was pretty hopeful that he'd have some sort of aptitude for police work.'

As appealing as Lloyd looked on paper, there was just one problem: SAPOL didn't actually need another police dog.

They already had two puppies being 'run on' – prepared for life as police dogs – in Victoria. One of those was set to be paired up with Senior Constable Tony Potter, whose current dog, five-year-old Ink, was facing early retirement due to degenerative arthritis. The other puppy would be a 'spare'.

In theory, police dogs usually retire from duty at between seven and eight years of age, but in Simon's experience it rarely works out that way.

'By the time a dog is about six we start thinking, *Okay, we're going to have to replace you in twelve to eighteen months,*' he says. 'But then a dog might get injured, or a handler might leave when the dog is six and a half – there's no point matching that dog with a new handler, so it'll be early retirement for the dog. We try to have at least one or two spares in the system.'

With a full complement of dogs and dogs-in-training, Lloyd was surplus to requirements – but Simon knew better than to let such an opportunity pass by.

'It wasn't crucial that we find a new dog, but we could use one if we did find one. And even if we met him and couldn't use him, there are always other police forces that we can help out.'

So he drove out to Windamere kennels to meet this 'problem child', Lloyd. First impressions were definitely positive.

'The first thing I noticed about Lloyd was that he was quite a large dog, and he was nice looking – pure black. He was very alert, which I liked,' says Simon. 'He was social, boisterous, playful – and that was out of his comfort zone. Sometimes dogs are confident in their own backyard, but this dog was already in an environment that was unfamiliar to him.'

Simon ran Lloyd through a series of basic tasks. He wanted to see if the dog had the key quality a police dog must possess: a high prey drive. Police dogs must want to chase, to follow their nose, to hunt and find their quarry.

Even as an untrained, nine-month-old rescue dog Lloyd was ticking every box.

'I'd throw something into the long grass so it was out of

sight and straight away he was using his nose to find it. It showed he had a hunt drive and work ethic,' Simon says. 'It wasn't just that he was happy to chase his favourite ball – he would chase anything, so that was really good.'

It wasn't just this instinctive behaviour that impressed Simon – for all his pent-up energy, Lloyd also seemed to have the perfect temperament for a police dog.

'He was very clear headed; a nice, stable dog. He was calm: focused on his toy but not over-the-top aggressive,' he says. Police dog training uses playtime with a favourite toy as a reward, so a certain degree of possessiveness over that toy is important.

Jacqui, Dennis and Sue looked on as Simon made his initial assessment. They couldn't believe how quickly Lloyd seemed to tune in to what Simon wanted from him.

'This dog was so intuitive. He worked for Simon straight away. We all just looked at each other and our jaws dropped,' Jacqui says. 'We could tell then that Simon was interested, and we were hopeful.'

Without wanting to make any promises to GSDRSA, Simon was impressed enough with Lloyd to ask to take him away from Windamere for further testing the following month.

In the back of his mind, Simon was thinking that Lloyd might be a better match for Tony Potter than one of the puppies waiting in the wings. Tony's dog, Ink, probably had another six months of active duty left in him at best – why not let Ink put his paws up now and have Tony wrangle Lloyd into shape instead?

Lloyd was brought to SAPOL's barracks at Thebarton in Adelaide's inner-western suburbs. Simon and Tony put him through his paces together.

'We want a police dog to be bold enough to go out in front of the handler. We want him to focus on the person in front of him, and we don't want him to turn away,' says Simon. 'I put a hoodie over my head and came out from behind this big dirt mound. Lloyd was standing there with Tony and straight away he was out, end of lead, watching me. His ears were up and he was growling: *I don't like this, you're unfamiliar to me.* All of that was exactly what we were looking for.'

The senior constables also took Lloyd to the site of the former Glenside psychiatric hospital. Its abandoned buildings would be a test of his willingness to work in dark, confined and frankly spooky settings.

'We routinely take prospective dogs to unfamiliar buildings to test their environmental stability with things like slippery floors, dark areas, stairs, and confined spaces to see if they have any serious fears or phobias,' he explains.

Lloyd certainly didn't – after all, he'd already endured more confinement and instability in his young life than most dogs. What did he have to be scared of now? He aced every challenge the officers threw at him.

'From there,' says Simon, 'it was a matter of going, "This dog could work out."'

Jacqui and Max were on holiday in Europe when she received a call from one of her GSDRSA colleagues.

'We got a message saying, "Sit down – SAPOL want to take Lloyd and put him through their next training program, and if he passes he'll be a police dog,"' Jacqui recalls. 'We'd seen his potential from the moment we met him. We just cried and cried and cried.'

Senior Constable Tony Potter says landing a job with the SAPOL dog unit is the police equivalent of 'being selected for the Australian cricket team.'

He had already been a police officer for nine years by the time he was employed as a police dog handler in 2009.

'It's a hard gig to get into and it's incredibly sought after. We call it the best gig in the department,' Tony says. 'When they're selecting people for the dog unit, they look for someone who's had a fair bit of street experience and can work on their own, because you're going to be on your own with the dog.'

SAPOL's dog handlers work a rolling five-week roster that includes daytime, evening and overnight shifts. Though it's the hardest on the body clock, the week of night shifts is the favourite for most handlers: crooks tend to be most active under cover of darkness, and the dogs' incredible senses are at their peak when the sun goes down.

'The hours of darkness are the best shifts for us – we jokingly call night shift week our Grand Final week,' says Tony. 'It's the one week out of our roster that you really get to see the dog at its best.'

It was during a night shift in June 2014 that Tony's then two-year-old dog, Ink, suffered the terrible injuries that ultimately led to his early retirement. Ink chased down an offender during a 2.30 a.m. ATM robbery at a suburban shopping centre. The man leapt into a parked car and slammed Ink repeatedly with the door, leaving the courageous canine with broken ribs, a punctured lung and a ruptured disc in his spine.

Though he was back at work within three months, Ink developed degenerative arthritis in his spine and SAPOL decided in conjunction with vets to retire him sooner rather than later. The man who injured Ink was the first person charged with causing harm to a working dog under tough new laws passed in December 2013.

Tony was still working with Ink and knew that one of the up-and-coming puppies in Victoria had been earmarked for him, so he wasn't overly interested when he first heard about a rescue dog that looked like he had the goods for police work.

Then his colleague, Simon, suggested Tony take a look at the young German Shepherd called Lloyd.

'Simon said he looked okay and was worth pursuing. He said, "While we're waiting for these dogs to come over from Victoria, can you have a look at this other dog, develop it a bit and see what you think?"'

All prospective general-purpose police dogs must complete a twelve-week training course before officially joining the police force. Once a handler is allocated a dog for the course, that's the dog he will work with in the field.

'The idea was that when the dogs arrived from Victoria, we would look at the personalities of all three dogs and the personalities of the handlers and try to make the best possible matches before starting the training,' Tony says.

So while Tony had been asked to see what he could do with Lloyd in the lead-up to the training course, no official decision had yet been made as to which officer would become Lloyd's handler. 'We'll always look at a dog, but 98 per cent of them don't cut it. There was no compulsion for me to take him on at that stage so I figured we had nothing to lose.'

When he met Lloyd, he was cautiously optimistic.

'He was a little bit skinny. He was quite light, like a greyhound, but he had a good frame – I could see that when he filled out a bit he'd be a big dog,' he says. 'He was a high-drive dog. He had plenty of energy, and unless you channel that energy it can be quite a handful.'

But when he came into the Thebarton barracks and went home with Tony (all police dogs live with their handlers) that cautious optimism quickly became outright excitement.

'Within forty-eight hours of having him at home I said to my wife, "He's a keeper." Straight away there was just something – I can't quantify it, it's just that little one per cent you see in a dog,' says Tony. 'He was very responsive to me, to my voice, from day one. I could tell he had a willingness to learn.'

He knew Lloyd would be an asset to any handler, but he couldn't deny he wanted the promising dog for himself.

'Even though I'd had my heart set on this other dog I thought, *I'm going to put my hand up and ask to hang onto him.*'

He didn't have to ask – Simon already knew that Tony and Lloyd would make a formidable policing partnership. 'Simon said, "Your bond is already strong, and to give that up and start again with another dog would be pointless,"' he says.

So it was official: Lloyd and Tony would be a team, and the two puppies would be allocated to other, equally capable dog handlers.

The first thing Tony did was change his new dog's name. Though he appreciated the symbolism of the name Lloyd, he couldn't imagine himself shouting it in the dead of night as his jet-black dog pursued a villain.

He decided to call him Jax. Surprisingly, the name is not a portmanteau of Jacqui and Max (though Jacqui admits she does like to jokingly claim the credit).

'I prefer short, sharp and shiny names. The reason I went with Jax was that I'd always wanted a dog called Max,' says Tony. 'It's a nice, strong name, if a little old fashioned. Things have changed a bit these days so I thought I'd give it a modern twist and go with Jax.'

Though excited about Jax's potential, seeing Ink forced to retire before his time was bittersweet for Tony. And even though he would remain with Tony forever, the transition from working dog to pet was tough for Ink, too.

'When I first got Jax, Ink was still my working dog in one half of the enclosure in the police car, with Jax alongside him. I'd get Ink out and work him and train him, and then get Jax out as well so he could mimic the older dog and get used to the routine,' he explains.

'Then the day came when that was it for Ink because we were going to start training Jax. I drove out of the yard one morning and he stayed home. That wasn't a good day for Ink.

'Everything we do with the dogs is about the work being the ultimate reward. The car was Ink's safe place, his happy place. For that to cease all of a sudden, it was an issue.'

But long-term, retirement has been good to Ink. His arthritis is greatly improved now that he's not dealing with the rigours of police work. Now seven years old, he spends his day lolling in the sunshine at Tony's place. Ink and Jax are great mates, but Tony always makes sure that he leaves Jax in the car for a few minutes when he arrives home from work so that Ink can have his undivided attention.

Tony and Jax had begun the SAPOL dog training course in December 2017. In March 2018, Jax and the two Victorian puppies, Arnie and Zac, officially became police dogs.

A police dog's key tasks include searching (both open areas and buildings), locating offenders and engaging those offenders if they don't comply with police instructions. Depending on the situation, that engagement might include chasing, cornering or even physically restraining a person.

'It's all about human odour. We're basically looking for people that are trying to avoid the police, and they go to great lengths to hide themselves. The dog is a great tool – we almost don't need eyes, because the dog will sniff them out,' Tony explains.

Though he was still only a year old when he graduated, Jax wasted no time hitting his stride in the field. Much of his work relies on his powerful scenting ability, but Jax also has another weapon in his arsenal.

'Jax has these massive, bat-like ears. His hearing is absolutely incredible – he can hear a pin drop two hundred metres away,' says Tony. 'I would never pick up on a slight rustle of someone behind a bush, but he will drag me off to a location and I'm sure he hasn't been following a scent.'

Just as Tony picked up on that unknown 'something' when he first met Jax, he says that moment when his brave dog zeroes in on a target has a similar intangible magic about it.

'Police dogs are hunters, and German Shepherds have a distinct genetic design to do this. Jax's body language changes when he starts to get into hunt mode. You can watch it build. If he gets a little hint of a scent it's hair-on-the-back-of-the-neck stuff,' he says.

'If that person is on the move and going yard to yard, when the dog gets that whiff he'll pull me out of my boots.'

The unofficial motto of the SAPOL dog squad – and probably police dog units the world over – is 'Trust your dog.' Even the most seasoned police officer feels trepidation when looking for potentially dangerous offenders, especially in the middle of the night, but a dog handler's trust in his canine counterpart is absolute.

That's why the bond between dog and handler is so crucial: the dog's protective instincts can literally mean the difference between life and death.

'I'd be a liar if I said I didn't feel fear or anxiety. There are a good number of times, especially if it's a crime of violence or you've been informed the offender may have a weapon, where you think, *It's just me and my dog out here*,' says Tony. 'Your dog won't let you down. If Jax is barking at that door or that industrial rubbish bin, I trust him.

'When [the offender] comes out it's just a sense of joy: I'm safe, the dog's safe, the dog has done this thing for me and together we've done this thing for the community.'

When a police dog collars a crook it's known as a 'win'. Jax only had a couple of wins in his first few months on the beat, but he was young and still developing his skills, so Tony had realistic expectations.

His first arrest came just two months after his graduation, when Jax located a man hiding in bushes on a building site in Adelaide's eastern suburbs. The man was carrying a torch, bolt cutters and gloves, and was subsequently charged with being unlawfully on the premises and going equipped to steal.

Jacqui cried happy tears when she learned of Jax's involvement in the man's arrest. To her, it was a team effort.

'It was just amazing. We couldn't have done anything with Jax if we didn't have people like Dennis and Sue supporting us, and Simon and SAPOL giving this dog the life he should have had,' she says. 'They all did all that for us just out of love for the breed.'

Around the sixth month of their pairing, Tony says 'it was like the penny dropped' for Jax. At the time of press, the crime-fighting crusaders had more than twenty wins under their respective caps.

'We kept persisting and we had some terrific wins. There's a bit of luck involved as well,' he says. 'It's my role as his handler to ensure Jax has the best opportunity to use his skills and have a success.'

Given the twists and turns in his life so far, it's easy to forget that Jax is still only three years old. Tony believes police dogs hit the peak of their abilities around the age of five, so Jax's best years are truly still to come.

'We pay $5000-plus for good dogs from good breeders. Jax's adoption fee was all of $450. He was the find of the decade,' he says.

All going well, Jax will work until he's at least seven. Tony will be sixty then and has a very specific goal for his retirement.

'If I can keep myself fit and healthy, and keep the dog fit and healthy, my personal dream would be that we retire together,' he says. 'I want to work up until his last shift, and we'll finish that shift and walk out of here together. I want to walk off into the sunset with my dog.'

Abandoned puppy to successful working dog would be a remarkable transformation for any canine, but it's perhaps particularly poignant in Jax's case. This is a dog that was let down by the person supposed to care for him his entire life. Even after he was rescued, the bonds he formed with people were necessarily short lived.

It would make sense if Jax were deeply mistrustful of humans. Who could blame him if he had no interest in protecting any of us? And yet he has forged an unshakeable bond with his handler, and together they help to make the world we live in a little bit safer.

There's no doubt that Jax took a circuitous route to fulfilling his destiny as a police dog, but it's undeniably where he belongs. His life could have been bleak indeed if not for a small army of people who collectively decided to take a chance on him.

Jax's story is miraculous in that it shows not only what incredible things rescue dogs are capable of, but also what happens when people believe that no dog belongs in the too-hard basket.

SAMMY

From lost in the wilderness to home four years later

It's a sad fact that dogs disappear every day. Though we do all we can to keep them close, some are nothing if not determined. They escape through holes in fences and abscond when the plumber leaves the gate open. They flee during thunderstorms and wander off when their owners aren't looking.

Most of the time, happily, lost dogs come back. Usually they turn up on the doorstep hours later, sheepish and tired. Sometimes good Samaritans deliver them to vets or shelters, where microchips and social media appeals help them find their way home.

But some lost dogs don't return, leaving heartbroken owners with no option but to hope their four-legged friend has forged a new life with somebody worthy.

And very rarely, a lost dog reappears with a survival story so amazing it can only be called a miracle.

An intrepid Queensland Labrador called Sammy was one of those dogs.

Sammy was the adored companion of Aubrey McCarthy and her daughter, Jamie, who live on the Sunshine Coast. Aubrey comes from a dog-loving family and all of her furry friends have lived to a ripe old age. Her childhood dog, Misha, was a 'Rhodesian ridgeback–everything mix' who was a stately thirteen when she passed away. Her first dog as an adult was Jessie the fox terrier mix, who is still going strong today at the age of eleven.

So when Aubrey adopted Sammy in 2010, she hoped for at least a decade of tail-wagging adventures and unconditional love.

Sammy came from Aubrey's aunt, Cheryl, whose own Labrador was the proud mum of a litter of puppies. Jessie was then about two years old and Aubrey wanted to add a large breed dog to her furry family.

'I grew up with big dogs and had always wanted one of my own, so we got Sammy,' Aubrey says. 'But Jessie was the boss – if Sammy went near Jessie's stuff he'd tell her off.'

Aside from the occasional spat with her canine sibling, Sammy fit right in – it was as though she had always been part of the family. She had a strong nurturing streak and was like a second mum to little Jamie.

'Sammy was very cheeky and always getting into trouble, but more loving than anything else. She absolutely loved Jamie – she just followed her around everywhere and they'd run amok together,' says Aubrey.

In August 2013, when she was three years old, Sammy's

maternal instincts went into overdrive when she gave birth to nine beautiful puppies. Aubrey remembers marvelling at the fact that Sammy had the precise number of nipples needed to feed her brood. (Female dogs usually have between eight and twelve nipples, though it is unusual for them to have an odd number; Sammy had eleven in total but two were undeveloped.)

The birth of the puppies had not been easy for Sammy. The litter was delivered via emergency caesarean section after Sammy went into labour several days early and her puppies became distressed in the womb.

She spent several days on cage rest at the local vet clinic, recovering from the surgery and bonding with her offspring. By the time Sammy and the pups were cleared to go home, Aubrey was more than ready for some drama-free time with her dog. Surely now they were home and dry.

Not quite. Instead, Sammy's health took a terrifying turn for the worse.

'As we took her out to the car from the clinic, all this blood suddenly poured from her caesarean incision. We were in the car park and Jamie had to run back inside and get the vet,' she says.

Sammy was rushed back into surgery and her wound was re-opened, while Aubrey and Jamie were sent home to endure a torturous wait for news.

'The vet rang me later and said, "Do you have rat bait at home?"' Aubrey recalls.

Sammy's internal bleeding was so severe that the veterinarian suspected she had been poisoned. Aubrey was horrified – and also certain there was no way Sammy could have ingested rat bait.

Rats are ubiquitous on the subtropical Sunshine Coast. They love warmth, shelter and abundant food and water, all of which are readily available in the humid hinterland where Aubrey lives. Homeowners commonly use poison to control the rat population. A baited rat will die within four to seven days of consumption.

Aubrey used rat baits in her ceiling, but with pets and a young child at home, she was vigilant about making sure the toxic lures were out of reach of curious kids and canines. She even searched her property every morning for droppings and bait pellets that may have been moved by the rats.

How on earth could Sammy have eaten rat bait? After some fairly disgusting detective work, Aubrey had her answer: Sammy hadn't eaten the bait.

She had eaten a *rat*.

'We checked her poo and there was fur in it. She'd obviously found the slow rat that had eaten the bait, and ate it,' she says.

Sammy must have swallowed her potentially lethal prey right before her puppies were born – perhaps the poisoned rat was even the catalyst for her early labour.

With the cause of her bleeding identified, Sammy's vet could act swiftly to save her life. She had lost so much blood that a donor dog was readied to provide a blood transfusion, but the vet was ultimately able to stanch the haemorrhage just before Sammy needed it. She was saved in the nick of time.

Her puppies had been given a dose of vitamin K as a precaution (a vitamin K deficiency can cause internal bleeding), but incredibly managed to survive the ordeal unscathed.

While Sammy convalesced at the clinic once more, Aubrey and Jamie took the nine puppies home. Sammy returned the following day, with instructions for a special diet and bed rest. She also brought with her a $5000 vet bill, which the clinic kindly allowed Aubrey to pay in installments over the next several months.

Sammy's milk didn't come in until day four. In the interim, Aubrey would wake every two hours to bottlefeed the litter, helping them to grow strong and healthy.

Sadly, one puppy didn't make it, likely as the result of a blood clot. The vet carried out an autopsy to check whether the little dog's death was related to the poisoning, but could find no link.

In the midst of the chaos, Aubrey took in a second Labrador, Nala, whose original owners decided she was getting too big. Though she wasn't yet a year old herself, Nala took on the role of surrogate mum, tirelessly taking care of Sammy's week-old puppies as best she could.

Sammy had narrowly escaped death twice in as many weeks. She had packed more stress into that fortnight than most dogs do in a lifetime. Aubrey was confident her calamity-prone dog had now more than met her lifetime crisis quota.

Alas, it wasn't to be, and Sammy would need a third miracle to make it through her next catastrophe.

*

If the warm spring afternoon on 27 October 2013, was any indication, Aubrey suspected summer that year would be a scorcher. She wondered if Nala would miss her regular outings to Wild Horse Mountain Lookout in the nearby Beerburrum East State Forest once the weather got too hot.

The 700-metre walk to the lookout was steep, and even the breathtaking 360-degree views at the top, spanning the Glass House Mountains to the west and Bribie Island to the east, couldn't persuade Aubrey and Jamie to make the trek when the temperature soared.

Nala was an easy dog to walk. Aubrey didn't need to hold tightly to her leash, because Nala never ventured more than a metre or two ahead.

'We were a two-minute drive from Wild Horse Mountain and we'd done that walk three or four times with Nala. We had no issues with her,' she says. 'Instead of her pulling us up the big hill, I'd drop her leash and let it trail on the ground and she'd stay with us.'

To her great chagrin, Sammy hadn't been allowed accompany her canine sister on the walks to the lookout so far. It had only been six weeks since her difficult delivery and close call with the rat bait. Aubrey didn't want to jeopardise Sammy's recovery, and also thought it wouldn't be fair to take her away from her puppies, which weren't yet fully weaned.

But on that lazy October Sunday afternoon, she relented. 'Sammy would always be at the gate when we got home from our walks to the lookout, waiting and looking sad because she couldn't come,' she says. 'On this day she was sulking at the fence when we were leaving so I thought, *Okay, you can come.*'

Sammy was overjoyed to be out in the fresh air with her family, and it showed.

'We did the leash thing and Sammy and Nala were about two metres ahead. Then they started playing sillybuggers and running off. We'd say, "Stop!" and they'd stop and look at us, and then as soon as we got near them they'd take off again.'

It was a great game – until it wasn't. After a few rounds of cat-and-mouse with their owner, Sammy and Nala didn't stop when Aubrey called. Instead of continuing up the mountain, the dogs darted off the concrete path into thick bush.

Aubrey wasn't immediately worried. She could hear the dogs crashing through the undergrowth, and every now and then would spot the mischievous pair among the trees not far from the path.

Then they disappeared from view.

'We were calling and they wouldn't listen, wouldn't come back. We thought they were just being naughty, so we kept walking for about a minute,' says Aubrey. 'Then we thought, *No, we'd better turn around because they aren't coming back.*'

Aubrey and Jamie headed down the hill to the car park. They were about halfway up the mountain at that stage, and fully expected to find Sammy and Nala waiting by the car, exhausted, when they got back.

'We turned back and came around the bend, and these tourists were walking up the mountain towards us with Nala. They said she'd just popped up on the path so they grabbed her leash and hoped they'd run into her owners,' she says. 'Nala didn't seem to care – she just thought it was all a fun game.'

Alarm bells started to ring for Aubrey when the tourists said they'd seen no sign of another dog.

Where on earth was Sammy?

'We expected her to be sitting by the car, buggered. When we got down to the bottom and she wasn't there, it was panic mode straight away. They should have been together.'

Together, Aubrey and Jamie spent twenty minutes searching the car park and surrounding bush, but Sammy was nowhere to be found. Then Aubrey thought she should drive the road that looped around the mountain and see if she could spot Sammy from the car.

But first she called for backup. 'I rang my Aunty Cheryl and said, "I can't find Sammy." She and my uncle were there within half an hour and we were all circling the mountain,' she says. 'I didn't know what to do. I'd never had a dog do that before.'

It was already close to four o'clock when Sammy went missing. Evening wasn't far away and Aubrey had to take Nala home and feed Sammy's puppies. But as night fell, she returned to Wild Horse Mountain to continue the search.

'We went back out again the next day and the next day and the next day, calling for Sammy . . . still nothing.'

Aubrey couldn't fathom how Sammy could simply vanish into thin air. The Beerburrum East State Forest is large – covering about 7700 hectares – but it is a popular destination for daytrippers, campers and locals. The busy Bruce Highway also bisects the forestry. Why hadn't anybody spotted her?

She posted increasingly frantic appeals for information on local community pages and lost pets groups on social media. She even contacted the organisers of a triathlon taking place in the forest to ask competitors to keep an eye out for Sammy.

After a few days, Aubrey was contacted by a woman who was involved with a local animal rescue group and had also trained her own dog in scent tracking.

'We'd been going round and round the mountain, and her concern was that it had already been three days and nobody was helping us. She was worried that Sammy could have gotten hurt,' Aubrey says.

'She got us to take her up the mountain to where we were when Sammy disappeared, and her dog went off the exact same way Sammy and Nala had gone. She said, "If she's here and she's injured or she's passed away, my dog will find her."'

The sniffer dog found no trace of Sammy, but Aubrey tried not to feel discouraged. As word spread about her missing dog, she was heartened by the number of complete strangers that joined her as she searched the forest.

'We had so many random people that ended up coming out and helping us look. I couldn't thank everyone enough,' she says. 'Whenever I was frustrated or it felt like everything was getting too much, they would be the ones running the Facebook page and setting up the search groups. I really thought we were going to find her.'

The search parties came tantalisingly close. On a couple of occasions, two separate groups of searchers heard a dog barking in the distance. Aubrey was in a different part of the forest each time and didn't hear it.

She and her family made several day trips to a spot where searchers had reported seeing fresh paw prints. They would cook a barbeque lunch each time, hoping the mouth-watering smell of frying sausages and onions would coax Sammy out of the bush. They even set a humane trap, but all they caught was a goanna.

Aubrey and her then partner also slept overnight in the forest one night. They took two of Sammy's puppies along, knowing what a devoted mum she was, and laid out food, water, and her puppies' blankets.

During another camping trip, Aubrey thought she was hallucinating when she spied a golden dog in the distance.

'It was her colour and size, and it went from one patch of bush to another across a dirt track. I called out Sammy's name, but this dog didn't stop,' she says. 'I was like, *I saw this dog, but it couldn't be Sammy because it didn't listen*. I wasn't sure if I was dreaming.'

After that encounter, Aubrey started to wonder if something awful had happened to Sammy that made her too scared to approach humans.

'People told me that sometimes lost dogs won't recognise their owners. Lots of people were giving us advice and telling us what could have happened.'

A few weeks into the search, Aubrey sought the guidance of an animal communicator – a sort of psychic for pets.

The woman described a ute and said its driver had picked Sammy up not realising she was lost. Aubrey managed to find the ute, but its owner didn't have Sammy.

She later consulted a further two animal psychics. One told her Sammy was indeed still in the forest and was being watched over by the spirit of Aubrey's late uncle.

'He always loved dogs, so that was a comfort,' she says.

The third psychic was based in New South Wales and had never been to the Beerburrum State Forest. She told Aubrey she felt that Sammy was still within 200 metres of where she was last seen. She said Sammy had found a safe place to sleep at night and spent her days making circuits of Wild Horse Mountain.

She also described the Bruce Highway and a road that passes under it. It was an area Aubrey was familiar with.

'My aunty went out there and came back saying, "You have to come and see what we've just found – there's fresh paw prints exactly where she said Sammy was,"' Aubrey says.

So the search shifted gear and focused intently on that area. Soon after, search HQ received a call from a truck driver who believed he had seen Sammy nearby at one o'clock in the morning.

'His wife had told him that when he stopped at the service station near the forestry at night he should go for a walk and keep an eye out for Sammy,' she says. 'He did, and said he saw a Labrador on a path around the area up where the trucks stop. It was only about five hundred metres from where we'd found the prints.'

The sightings were encouraging, but also frustrating for Aubrey. She couldn't understand why Sammy would apparently reveal herself to strangers, yet avoided all of Aubrey's attempts to catch so much as a glimpse of her beloved dog.

'I was thinking, *Why are all these people seeing her and I'm not? She's* my *dog!* So much happened and so many people tried to help, but every time we felt we were getting closer it just never happened,' she says.

As time dragged on, Sammy's absence began to take a toll on Aubrey's mental health. For more than three months, she had searched for her dog day and night. The search became a full-time job. In fact, she had left her real job because her employer wouldn't accommodate the time off she needed to care for Sammy's puppies. Aubrey also had Jessie and Nala at home, plus Sammy's nine puppies to care for, not to mention her own daughter, Jamie.

'Jamie was only three at the time, but she did understand what was happening and she was really upset,' says Aubrey. 'Not so much for the first couple of days, but going on after that she was like, "I don't know if we're going to find her."'

There were days when Aubrey felt completely hamstrung by the situation: she didn't know if she had the strength to continue, but she knew she would never forgive herself if she called off the search altogether.

'I don't think I ever really gave up, but eventually the search slowed right down,' she says. 'I pretty much lost the plot. I was like, *I can't do it anymore*. I just thought I wasn't going to find her, but I couldn't give up either.'

Aubrey continued to return to the forest and look for Sammy whenever she could, and always followed up on any lead or reported sighting, but at the same time she tried to move on with her life for the sake of her family and their remaining pets.

'I was at a water park one New Year's Day when I got a message from a lady who was out in the forest four-wheel driving. She heard leaves rustling and could tell that something had just run off, and her partner said he saw a dog that looked like Sammy,' she says. 'We'd hear something like that and then we'd spend the next two weeks out there, searching.

'People would always tag me in "found dog" posts on social media. I still always looked, but it was never her.'

Compounding her anguish was a shocking family tragedy. On Anzac Day in 2016, Aubrey's sister, Gemma, died unexpectedly. She was heavily pregnant, and the double loss devastated Aubrey and her family.

'Gemma always approved and was proud of how far I went to find Sammy,' she says.

The months turned into years. Suspected Sammy sightings became sparse. Aubrey grieved for Gemma and tried to face the grim likelihood that her death-defying dog's luck had finally run out – and worse, that she would never know what had happened to Sammy.

And then, on 22 April 2017, Aubrey was tagged in yet another 'found dog' post on Facebook. Sammy had been gone for three-and-a-half years. It couldn't be her.

Could it?

*

Aubrey could barely keep up with the emails and texts. Since the first person had tagged her in a post about a filthy and injured dog that had been found in the forest that morning, she had received a stream of messages from people convinced the forlorn creature was Sammy.

Aubrey wasn't nearly so certain. She had last seen Sammy as a boisterous three year old; she would be seven by now. The dog in the pictures seemed to be older and didn't look like the bundle of fluff Aubrey remembered. She'd simply been through too much and had her hopes dashed too many times to dare to dream this dog was her lost Lab.

Nevertheless, she agreed to speak to the coordinator of a Facebook lost pets page, where staff at a local vet hospital had posted the information about the found dog.

But when the call came, Aubrey found she didn't have the strength to take it.

'I asked my mum to take the call instead because at that point I was still thinking, *I don't know, I don't think it's Sammy*,' she recalls. 'But mum spoke to the lady and then said, "I think it might be her."'

The woman said the dog had been picked up by a young couple staying in a campervan at a campground known locally as the Rustic Cabin; she had simply materialised from out of the bush and approached them. The sad creature had a gory leg wound and seemed to be in pain, so the couple put her in their van and took her to the closest vet, which happened to be twenty minutes away at Caloundra.

The clinic's social media posts explained how the pooch had caught the eye of Sammy's army of searchers.

The Rustic Cabin is in the Beerwah State Forest, about half an hour from where Sammy went missing. Beerwah is connected to the Beerburrum State Forest, but it's on the other side of the bustling Bruce Highway. If this dog was indeed Sammy, she had somehow dodged cars and semi-trailers hurtling along at 110 kilometres per hour to cross a four-lane motorway.

Aubrey told her mum to ask the caller whether the dog had a noticeable caesarean scar; Sammy's was particularly prominent because of the second life-saving surgery she'd had after eating the poisoned rat. When the woman on the phone said the dog did indeed have a scar, Aubrey felt her heart soar in spite of her misgivings.

But she came crashing down to earth a moment later when she asked if the dog had a microchip. Sammy did – but the found dog didn't.

Still, she felt she had to go to the clinic to see the dog. Only then would she truly know if it was her Sammy.

'We went into the vet and saw her and I was still like, *I don't know*. It wasn't like I immediately went, "That's her!" I felt it could be, but if it was she had changed – it was four years later and she looked so much older,' says Aubrey.

The poor dog was also extremely dirty and smelled awful, and the wound on her front right leg was gruesome to say the least. She also had severe ear infections, rotten teeth and her toenails were long and curled. But she certainly did have the scar Aubrey remembered, as well as nine developed and two undeveloped nipples.

Young Jamie, who was by now seven as well, didn't need any convincing. 'Jamie thought it was Sammy straight away,' Aubrey says. 'She had always missed her. We didn't have Sammy's collar because she had it with her when she got lost, but we'd got another collar exactly the same just for something to have.'

The evidence seemed to suggest it was Sammy – but much as she hoped for a lightning bolt of recognition, Aubrey just couldn't say for sure.

'The clinic staff said they'd give her a bath so she looked and smelled better. Mum and I went to have a cup of coffee so I could have some time to think,' she says.

She also made a phone call to her Aunty Cheryl. Sammy was a big fan of Cheryl, who would often call in at Aubrey's house on her way home from work to say hello to the friendly Labrador. She had a habit of carrying her car keys in her hand, and to Sammy their jangling sound was a signal.

'The keys were a big thing: when Sammy heard the keys it'd be like, "Cheryl's here!" and she'd be jumping up at the fence to say hello,' says Aubrey.

Cheryl had made sure to have her keys in hand every time she ventured into the forest during the long months of searching for Sammy.

Aubrey and her mum went back to the clinic to spend some more time with the dog, who was by now clean and smelled fresh. Cheryl arrived soon afterwards.

'She was lying on the floor when Cheryl came in the door with her keys in her hand, and she got up and went straight to her,' she says. 'That really made it click. I was 99 per cent sure by then that it was Sammy, but as soon as she did that I was certain.'

Sammy was home. Against all the odds, she had made it back to her family after almost four years lost and alone in the wilderness – older and not in the best shape, but in one piece. If surviving the difficult birth of her puppies and a near-fatal poisoning had been amazing, this was truly a miracle.

But just *how* had she survived out there for so long? One theory was that Sammy had subsisted on pineapples pilfered from local farms. The poor state of her teeth supported the idea: the fruit's high acidity can weaken tooth enamel and cause decay.

Aubrey thinks a more likely cause of Sammy's dental issues is that she chewed on rocks in a bid to stave off hunger. She probably survived on small animals and water from creeks (this is a dog that could catch and eat a rat, after all).

If someone had picked Sammy up, as one of the psychics suggested early on in the search, she may even have damaged her teeth by trying to escape.

'I'm still not certain she survived on pineapples. Her regular vet said that when dogs are caged they will chew the bars,' says Aubrey. 'It does happen that wild dogs eat pineapples, but we just don't know.'

Sammy's missing microchip was also something of a mystery, but they have been known to move around under a pet's skin.

Amid the joy of finding her dog, Aubrey couldn't help wondering why it had taken so long. The spot where Sammy approached the campers wasn't all that far from where dozens of people had spent months looking for her. She *must* have seen or heard the search parties – why hadn't she come approached someone earlier?

She suspects it was fear that drove Sammy to remain concealed in the bush. 'The vet said she would have been in pain with her leg and had finally given up and realised she needed help,' she says.

However it was that Sammy managed to fend for herself for so long, Aubrey was ecstatic that she would never have to do it again. She couldn't wait to take Sammy home, nurse her back to health and spoil her for years to come.

She wondered if her sister had somehow had a hand in bringing Sammy back to her. 'Three days before the first anniversary of Gemma passing away was when Sammy came home,' she says. 'I do feel she helped with this.'

Sammy was overjoyed to be home, too. 'She would follow us around wherever we went. We were living with my mum at the time, and if I went to work Sammy would be under Mum's feet.'

Sammy's grisly leg injury was still healing – she'd had surgery to clean it up and was treated with antibiotics – but Aubrey was a diligent nurse, changing her dressing at home when Sammy managed to pull it off and making the thirty-minute trip to the vet every second day for new bandages.

It was at one of these routine vet visits that Aubrey was faced with horrifying news. The vet was concerned that Sammy's wound was more sinister than first suspected.

'Once it started healing I thought, *Great!* But it was only once it started to heal that it showed its true form. The vet was pretty sure it was cancer,' she says.

A biopsy confirmed the terrible diagnosis. Sammy had cancer in her leg, and given the extent of the disease her vets were sure it would already have spread to other organs.

The vets advised against amputating Sammy's leg, because dogs carry about 60 per cent of their weight on their front legs and don't tend to function well with a missing front limb.

All Aubrey could do was keep Sammy comfortable and smother her with as much love as possible in the time she had left.

Just as they had rallied when Sammy was missing, people wrapped both Sammy and Aubrey in love and support.

I didn't have money. I had nothing,' she says. 'All these people came with donations of beds and toys and blankets. Some ladies bought her these fancy new coats. A few of her followers finally got to meet her. It was beautiful.'

On 14 May 2017, just twenty-two days after she came home, Sammy let Aubrey know she was ready to go.

It was Mother's Day.

'People said, "You can't do that to yourself on Mother's Day," but I said, "No, I can't do that to *her.*" She was in so much pain that she couldn't even rest comfortably, and I couldn't let her suffer,' Aubrey says.

'I just can't believe that she came home. She spent all that time out there and finally made her way home to me.'

Sammy's survival for four years in the wilderness was incredible, but maybe the true miracle was her farewell. She overcame tremendous adversity to return to her family, and ended her life peacefully and pain free, cocooned in their love.

May we all be as lucky as Sammy.

MOLLY

From three years to live to foster family matriarch

There are certain things that even the most inexperienced dogparents know to expect when a new puppy joins the family. Chewing, for example – there will undoubtedly be a lot of that. Hide the good cushions and fancy shoes! The occasional 'accident' in the house is also a certainty while the pup gets to grips with peeing in the great outdoors. Expect to spend hours researching the most nutritious diet for young Fido, too. And then there's the healthy dog's to-do list: worming, vaccinations, desexing, and taking out a pet insurance policy.

What no dog owner ever anticipates is being blindsided by a diagnosis of a life-limiting illness in a twelve-week-old bundle of fluff. No dog owner imagines praying for a miracle to save their dog's life. But that's exactly what happened to Sharon Calder in 2009.

Sharon, from Perth in Western Australia, was far from a

novice dog owner when she bought her purebred Rottweiler puppy, Molly, from a registered breeder. She has loved dogs all her life, and has stood by her canine companions through good times and bad.

The first dog she fell in love with was her family's pet Border Collie, Lassie. 'She was the family dog, but I spent a lot of time with her when I was a child, walking and playing with her,' Sharon says. 'She got quite mangy and lost a lot of her fur, but she lived to be about fifteen.'

As an adult, Sharon shared another Border Collie, Bo, with her partner at the time. A few months later they added a German Shepherd puppy, Gemma, to the pack. Her relationship ended, but her love for her dogs never did. Bo, Gemma and Sharon were inseparable until Bo passed away from cancer at the age of ten.

Not long after Bo died, Sharon brought home Tasha, another Border Collie. Then she decided the time was right to fulfill her childhood dream of having a Rottweiler.

'I'd always wanted a Rottweiler, because when I was a kid my aunt and her kids had one and I just really loved it,' she says. 'I had never felt the time was right, because Rotties are super intelligent and can be naughty and stubborn, and I wanted to make sure I had my own house and lots of time to spend with a puppy before I made that decision.'

It was actually Gemma that helped Sharon decide she had room in her home – and her heart – for another dog. By the autumn of 2009, her faithful German Shepherd was nearly sixteen and in poor health. In the last year of her life Gemma developed canine cognitive dysfunction, also known as 'doggy dementia'. Symptoms include confusion or disorientation, anxiety and restlessness, irritability and a sudden inability to follow familiar routines. Sharon knew it wouldn't be long before her girl let her know she was ready to go. She hoped having a new puppy would ease her grief when the time came, as well as help Tasha to cope with the inevitable loss of her longtime companion.

Sharon thoroughly researched local registered Rottweiler breeders, and when she found one with available puppies she did all the things buyers of pedigree dogs are advised to do. She met the parents, she checked that the puppies had been screened for inherited health issues such as hip and elbow dysplasia, and she visited several times before choosing the pup she felt was right for her. She decided to name her new four-legged friend Molly.

'There were only four puppies in the litter. I wanted a female and there were only two. I don't know what it was in particular, why I picked her – I think I just felt more of a bond with her,' Sharon says.

Just a couple of months after Sharon brought Molly home, Gemma passed away. It was as if she had waited to meet the little dog that would be by Sharon's side when she no longer could. Sharon, Tasha and Molly were a unit now, and she looked forward to many happy years with her dogs.

But none of her careful groundwork could prepare Sharon for what came next.

When Molly was twelve weeks old, Sharon took the apparently healthy, energetic puppy to the vet for her second round of core vaccinations. These inoculations against dangerous diseases including distemper and parvo are given at six, twelve and sixteen weeks.

When the vet placed his stethoscope to Molly's chest, his face fell. He could hear a whooshing sound, and knew immediately that Molly had a heart murmur.

A vet should be able to hear two sounds from a healthy heart: a 'lub' and a 'dub'. These are the sounds of the heart's valves closing as blood flows through them. Any extra noise, such as a whoosh, suggests the blood is not flowing properly; the turbulent flow of the blood is what creates the sound.

Vets rank the severity of a heart murmur from one to six, with one being barely audible and six being the loudest. A level six murmur can sometimes even be felt with a hand on the chest, without the aid of a stethoscope.

In dogs, common causes of heart murmurs include valve problems, heart defects, heartworm disease, tumours or weakening of the heart muscle. But while a heart murmur can indicate a serious condition, it isn't always cause for concern. Many dogs with mild heart murmurs experience no ill effects, and murmurs in puppies are relatively common – they often disappear as the dog grows and ages.

Sharon fervently hoped that would be the case for her much-loved puppy. She was young and full of life: if any dog was going to fall into the 'best case scenario' category, surely it was Molly.

Sadly, the news was grave. Further investigation revealed Molly's heart murmur was caused by subaortic stenosis, an incurable disease that occurs most commonly in large-breed dogs. The aortic valve sits between the heart's left ventricle and the aorta, the largest artery in the body. Subaortic stenosis occurs when the area underneath the aortic valve narrows, causing some degree of blockage of blood flow through the heart. (It also occurs less frequently in the valve itself, and very rarely in the area above the valve.)

The narrowing can be mild, moderate or severe. If the disease is mild, it usually has little to no effect on the dog and no treatment is required. But if it is moderate or severe, it forces the heart to work harder and can increase the dog's risk of fainting, collapse and even sudden death.

To Sharon's utter dismay, Molly's condition was classified as being at the high end of the moderate range. Within six months, it had progressed to severe.

Sharon was stunned. Her longed-for little dog, not even a year old, seemed to be facing a bleak future. There was no gentle way for the vet to deliver Molly's grim prognosis.

If she lived beyond the age of three, he said, it would be a miracle.

In an instant, all the plans Sharon had for Molly and their life together went out the window. She had intended to sign up for obedience and agility training, and looked forward to taking Molly swimming at the beach and running around at the dog park.

None of that seemed possible now. Molly's life would likely be short, and involve lots of expensive vet visits. She might struggle with weakness, breathing difficulties and fainting. Eventually she would need daily medication.

Moderate and severe subaortic stenosis is most commonly treated with beta blockers, medication that reduces blood pressure. They help to ease the heart's workload by preventing it from beating too fast.

Molly's vet also advised Sharon to report the puppy's diagnosis to the breeder, as subaortic stenosis is thought to be a genetic condition. Responsible breeders will always take a dog back if the owner is unable to care for it, but the thought of returning Molly never entered Sharon's mind.

'I never once thought about giving her back to the breeder. I'd already had her for five weeks when she was diagnosed. She was mine and that was all there was to it,' she says. 'We do have a very special bond.'

What Sharon *did* do, however, was promise Molly that she would do everything in her power to help keep her as happy and healthy as possible for as long as she could.

'On walks she would lag behind after about ten minutes, then run around like crazy in the backyard and I'd have to stop her,' she says. 'The vet said dogs with this condition will normally just die suddenly from heart failure, so I made a decision that I would monitor Molly's exercise and not let her get so worked up that her heart could stop.'

That meant no swimming off leash in open water, no long walks and no rough-and-tumble with other dogs at the park. Instead, Sharon connected with other local dog owners online and set up one-on-one play dates with other dogs, allowing Molly to socialise safely in a controlled environment.

At home, Sharon made sure she was always by Molly's side. 'She's literally never outside unless I'm with her, because if I'm with her I can keep her calm. Whenever I'm not home she stays in the house,' she explains.

It was even too risky to have Molly desexed, because anaesthesia and surgery would place too much strain on her heart.

With Sharon's care and vigilant supervision, along with a healthy raw diet and regular check-ups at the vet, the months soon turned into years. Before long it was 2012, and Molly's third birthday was approaching. It was a tense time for Sharon, who had the vet's predicted three-year 'deadline' constantly on her mind.

And yet Molly was happy and thriving. She didn't seem like a dog nearing the end of her life. Could she prove the experts wrong and survive beyond the age of three? Would Sharon get the miracle she so desperately wanted?

She did. Molly turned three in April, and then kept right on going.

'It was really stressful until she turned three because the vet had said that number. It was like this massive weight had lifted all of a sudden,' she says. 'Every year I'm just astonished when she has another birthday.'

Not long after reaching that miraculous milestone, Molly went into heat. When a female dog is not desexed, she goes into heat for about three weeks every six months or so. If she were to mate during this period, she would likely become pregnant. There was no chance Molly was pregnant – dogs with subaortic stenosis should not be bred, and Sharon would never take that risk – but Molly certainly thought she was.

She was in the grip of a false, or phantom, pregnancy. Research shows the majority of female dogs will show signs of false pregnancy after a heat cycle, regardless of whether or not they were mated. Physical signs include mammary gland swelling, milk production, lethargy, vomiting and fluid retention. Behavioural changes include nesting, restlessness and mothering activities. Some dogs will even go into false labour.

It wasn't much fun for Molly, and it was just as hard for Sharon to watch. 'She was producing milk, and getting toys and putting them against her belly. It was really heartbreaking,' she recalls.

After much discussion with her vet, Sharon decided to have Molly desexed after all. Now that she'd made it to three, the benefits seemed to outweigh the risks. The plucky pooch had beaten all the odds stacked against her so far, and Sharon didn't want her to have to suffer through phantom pregnancies twice a year for the rest of her life.

Still, despite assurances from her vet that Molly would be fine, the day of her surgery was a tough one for Sharon. 'It took a lot of convincing from my vet that she'd be okay and they wouldn't let her die,' she says. 'I was a bit of a mess that day until they rang me to say she was okay.'

While being spayed meant Molly's body would no longer trick her into believing she was pregnant, watching her lovingly nurture her toys had got Sharon thinking. Sharon wondered if bringing a younger dog into Molly's life might allow her to indulge her innate maternal urges.

Sharon got in touch with the animal rescue group

Saving Perth Animals from Euthanasia. Better known as SAFE Perth, the no-kill rescue doesn't have a shelter, but instead a network of foster carers who take in stray and surrendered pets in need of a temporary place to stay while they wait to be adopted into forever families.

Sharon signed up to foster. 'It wasn't something I'd necessarily planned. I started fostering because Molly really loves other dogs, and she was going through these feelings because of the phantom pregnancy. I just thought, *I'll foster some puppies for her*,' she says.

'Our first fosters were two puppies through SAFE. Molly loved it, because she loved caring for them. She actually likes other dogs coming onto her property, whereas dogs often don't because they're territorial. I've been fostering ever since so that she's got new dogs to play with.'

In the seven years since those first two pups found permanent homes, Sharon and Molly have fostered more than twenty dogs and puppies.

That's right: *seven* years. Molly, the desperately ill puppy that wasn't expected to make it to her third birthday, is now ten years old.

Perhaps due to her own health problems, the gentle Rottie seems to have a special affinity for so-called 'problem' dogs. Many of her foster friends have had significant physical or behavioural issues and would not have coped well in a shelter or pound environment; if these dogs hadn't found a foster home, they would likely have been euthanised. But with Molly to guide them, they have blossomed into loving and adoptable family pets.

She simply adores being the matriarch of her big, crazy family. 'She's very, very good with other dogs. Some of the dogs we've fostered have been deemed dog aggressive, but Molly is very calm with them – she knows when to back off,' says Sharon. 'She's just a really good role model for them.'

Some of the foster dogs have done so well in Molly's company that they became 'foster fails' and stayed permanently. One was an Australian shepherd mix called Missy, who was ten years old when Sharon spotted her picture on a rescue website. Missy's owner had died and she was one of three dogs surrendered to the pound at Northam, north-east of Perth, by the family.

'It was a terrible situation. She was in a tin pound on a 40-degree day and I drove ninety minutes to go pick her up the next day just to get her out of there,' she recalls. 'She had a thick coat and it was really matted because she'd been so neglected. The night I got her home I brushed her, and after brushing for a while I found a collar under that matted coat.'

Missy lived with Sharon, Molly and Tasha for two years before she developed a serious autoimmune disease in 2013 and Sharon had to make the heartbreaking decision to have her put to sleep.

Six months before Missy passed away, Sharon had taken Banjo into foster care. He was an elderly Shar Pei–Staffordshire Bull Terrier mix who had worn out his welcome at four other foster homes in the space of a month.

'Banjo was at least ten, maybe twelve, and in really bad shape in terms of aggression. I think he must have been left out in a backyard, chained up. He had a lot of anxiety and was on medication, and he just wasn't going to be able to be rehomed, so I thought we'd give him a go,' she says.

Banjo had a real problem with resource guarding: for the first several months he lived with Sharon, he would try to attack any other dog that ventured near his bed. He wouldn't share a water bowl. He even broke a window and escaped once. 'After about three months he started to realise that no one was going to hurt him or steal his stuff. Molly would lie with him, but she would never try to play with him,' she says.

When Sharon went out, Banjo had to be separated from Molly and the other dogs because Sharon simply couldn't predict what he would do. Then one day she decided to let the whole pack stay together while she went to work. When she returned, the house was peaceful. It was as if Banjo finally understood that he was part of a family.

After Missy died, Sharon formally adopted Banjo, making him her second foster fail. When he died in late 2015, he was probably around fourteen years old. She suspected he'd known more love, patience and kindness in the two years he spent with her, Molly, Tasha and Missy than in the entirety of his life before then.

'I've learned a lot about dog behaviour through fostering. A lot of the time, I don't think "aggressive" dogs really are aggressive. They've been taken from one home and put in a new home with new people and new dogs,' she says. 'I think they're just reacting to a stressful situation.'

Cypher the white German Shepherd also arrived as an emergency foster care case in 2016 and never left. He and

Molly bonded instantly, and he was a great comfort to her when Tasha passed away later that year at the age of twelve.

'He's a really lovely dog, so I just kept him. He's quite vocal – he likes the sound of his own voice and he sings-slash-yells in this high-pitched voice,' Sharon laughs. 'Cypher and Molly love each other – you'd think they were together as littermates.'

Sharon believes sharing her home with foster siblings has been a big factor in Molly's longevity. So puppy-like is her behaviour, it's easy to forget about her heart condition.

'I don't even think about it anymore. She's so mischievous. It's like living with a two year old! She opens doors and even tries to turn the key because she's seen me do it. She'll go around and look in drawers because she just wants to see what's in there,' she says. 'I've got a spa and she'll jump in and out in a single leap. She splashes around and bites the water. One of my cupboards doesn't shut properly and she'll stand there and bang it just to be annoying. She's hilarious.'

Molly clearly isn't aware that she's not well. Sometimes Sharon's vow to keep Molly calm and quiet is not at all easy to maintain. 'She's got so much energy and she still tries to run around. She'll go racing down the backyard and I'm like, "Argh!" But I have to let it happen. There's no point wrapping her in cotton wool.'

Every day since Molly's diagnosis has felt like an unexpected bonus, but in early 2018 Sharon was reminded of just how serious her dog's health issues are. A vet check-up revealed Molly's subaortic stenosis is now off the charts – so severe that none of the existing veterinary classifications apply anymore. She now takes beta blockers twice a day.

Every extra minute they get together now feels like another mini miracle, says Sharon. 'Her condition is very severe. There's not even a word for it. The specialist vet called her an anomaly. It seems from the way they're talking that they're thinking, *How is her heart even still beating?*'

Sharon has decided to press the pause button on fostering for the time being. Molly has shared so much of herself for so long that Sharon feels she deserves some quiet time with just her and her best friend, Cypher.

She is determined to fill Molly's remaining time with as many 'bucket list' experiences as possible – albeit in the sedate style Molly has come to expect.

'After I found out how bad her heart is now, I took Molly and Cypher to Dwellingup, in the south-west of WA, where there's a big lake,' she says. 'I got her a life vest so she could just swim around as much as she wanted.'

Sometimes Sharon thinks about what her life would look like if she'd never bought Molly. It might have been a little less stressful. She probably would have pursued different opportunities, like job offers that involved travel – she happily turned them down because she never wanted to be away from Molly.

But she doesn't spend too much time wondering what might have been, because a life without Molly would have been a life without joy, without laughter, and without the incredible transformations of the dogs she and Molly have helped.

'I probably never would have fostered if it weren't for Molly. The reality is there's all these small, non-funded rescue groups that do 90 per cent of the work in Australia, and I wouldn't have known they existed,' says Sharon. 'The majority of my friends now are rescue people that I never would have met if it wasn't for her.'

Nor does she waste precious time thinking about what life might have been like for Molly if she'd been born with a healthy heart.

'I used to feel sorry for her because I thought, *I'd love to be able to take you to the beach and things*. It's not that she couldn't do it, but I just didn't want to take the risk if I could prevent it,' Sharon says. 'But I've never felt like she's missed out on things, because I really have made an effort to give her the best life.'

There's no two ways about it: Molly is a medical miracle. But what's even more miraculous about her long life is that, as a dedicated 'foster sister', she has spent it nurturing and saving the lives of other dogs. They are dogs that had been tossed in the too-hard basket; dogs that would have faced very bleak futures indeed had they not had Molly to guide them.

Her heart may be ailing, but it is positively bursting with love. What an incredible gift.

BILLY

From critically ill to national obedience champion

If you pop in to visit the Braes clan at home in the Queensland port city of Gladstone, 550 kilometres north of Brisbane, there are a few things that are sure to catch your eye.

You'll see the usual cheerful clutter of a family with three children – Kaiden, five, and Katie, eleven, are at primary school, while eldest daughter Racie is at university – and if you're lucky you'll get a glimpse of Marli the cat.

You can't fail to notice the impressive interior décor: the walls are hung with ribbons, plaques and certificates, which represent the multitude of canine obedience competitions that homeowner Frank Braes has won with his dogs over the years.

But it's the mantelpiece in the living room that will really intrigue you – or more accurately, what's *on* the mantelpiece. There is a small pine box bearing the inscription

Feluga Bound for Glory, along with a photograph of a handsome Staffordshire terrier. Next to the box is a clear plastic Ziploc bag, inside which is a well-chewed blue tennis ball.

These apparently innocuous artifacts represent the best and worst of times for the Braes family. One marks the end of a remarkable life, while the other is proof that miracles happen every day. They are testament to the emotional highs and lows that we all sign up for when we open our hearts to a dog.

Frank knows that rollercoaster well. He has loved dogs his whole life, and they have put him through the wringer on more than one occasion.

The first four-legged friend to leave a mark on his heart was the whimsically named Ding Dong, who wandered into the yard of Frank's childhood home at Mareeba in Far North Queensland in the 1970s and simply never left.

'He was an old Labrador cross and he was covered in fleas and ticks. Mum and Dad just kept him,' says Frank. 'He used to sit on the front stairs of the house and that was all he did. That was my first experience of dogs.'

His next canine companion was a little more energetic. Snoopy was a black-and-white fox terrier who technically belonged to Frank's older sister, Jenni. When she left home, Snoopy stayed behind, and after Frank's father passed away in 1988, Snoopy forged a strong bond with Frank and his mum.

When Snoopy too reached the end of his life, Frank felt his loss deeply.

'He really became our dog. He never had a tablet or anything in his life and lived to be about thirteen,' he says. 'He was buried under an orange tree in the yard of that house.'

By the time he was in his late teens, Frank had started a job laying floor coverings. A chance encounter on a job one day would spark a lifelong love affair.

'I went out to this farm and got out of the truck and saw this dog that had a massive big head. I'd never seen one like it before,' says Frank, who now works as a labourer.

He spoke to the dog's owner, who told Frank the sturdy pooch was a Staffordshire Bull Terrier. The dog was missing some fur from the top of his head, and Frank asked what had happened.

'The owner said his .22 rifle had accidentally gone off and ricocheted off the dog's head,' he recalls.

Frank didn't need to hear another word: he was instantly sold on the breed. 'I said to myself, "I want one of those dogs – they're so tough!"'

The Staffordshire Bull Terrier – or Staffy, as the breed is commonly known – is a medium-sized dog that developed in England in the nineteenth century. Stocky and muscular, with a broad head and perpetually wagging tail, Staffies are thought to descend from bull and terrier-type dogs bred for the blood sports of dog fighting and rat baiting.

Baiting and organised dog fighting were outlawed in the UK in 1835, and Staffies have been wildly popular companion dogs for the nearly 200 years since. In the UK they were even nicknamed 'nanny dogs', such was their reputation as a playmate and protector of children. The breed is intelligent and highly trainable, and known for being gentle, fun loving and easygoing.

It wasn't long before Frank had a Staffy of his own, but the black-and-white puppy he bought in 1991 didn't bear much resemblance to the bullet-dodging beast he'd encountered at the farm.

Rebel – or Feluga Bound for Glory, to use his pedigree name – was the runt of his litter. 'I didn't choose a Staffy because I wanted an aggressive or scary-looking dog. Rebel was very small and had fur missing off him,' says Frank. 'He was a really good dog – the best-natured dog I've ever owned.'

As Rebel got older and filled out a bit, Frank hoped to turn the handsome dog into a show ring champion.

Alas, it wasn't to be. A freak accident that saw Rebel break his two back legs when he was a puppy put paid to his show career before it had even begun. More than two decades later, Frank still berates himself for inadvertently causing Rebel's injuries.

'I was walking down near the creek with him and there was a little skinny bridge. He wouldn't have been able to walk over it, so I picked him up and sort of gently tossed him to the other side,' he says.

'I didn't realise that when Staffies are really young their bones are like toothpicks and they don't have the muscles to support them. He ended up having three pins in each leg and the vet told me his legs probably wouldn't last past the age of seven.

'But even after that he was up and walking around the next day. The vet said, "Make sure he rests" and I said, "How do you suggest I do that?"'

Determined to prove the vet's grim prediction wrong, Frank started looking for an activity that would help to keep Rebel active and limber for as long as possible. His healed back legs were a little too wonky for the show circuit, but Frank wasn't about to write off a dog that was barely a year old.

He found what he was looking for in obedience trialling.

All pet dogs need basic obedience training, but the sport of obedience trialling kicks things up a notch. There are five levels of competition obedience in Australia, and different classes from novice through to master.

Each level is progressively more challenging for both dog and owner, and state and national titles can be won at each level. Most levels require a pass of 170 points or more out of 200 at three separate trials, and the dog must pass every exercise within the level. (The exception is the Community Companion Dog title, which is the basic level of competition and requires a minimum 85 points out of 100.)

All the exercises are based on useful things dogs can do for humans, and which make for a better companion, such as walking to heel off lead, recall and sit-stay.

Frank and Rebel took to obedience trialling like pros, though competing for titles wasn't initially part of the plan.

'We travelled 35 kilometres every Thursday to do this training, and Rebel was getting a lot of accolades within the club, but I got a bit lazy,' Frank says. 'I was just going there week after week and one of the leaders of the club finally said, "We're going to book you in for some trials." They entered me into an upcoming trial, and I'm glad they did.'

Almost immediately, Rebel started winning titles, even setting records at some levels. He averaged 190 out of 200 points at various trials over the course of his career.

'We never looked back. Rebel won first place in everything he went in. There may even be some records still standing,' he says.

Rebel excelled in obedience trialling in the region for more than a decade. Sadly, he became ill at the age of thirteen and passed away in 2004. Even though the tenacious dog had miraculously walked six years longer than veterinarians had predicted, the loss was still utterly devastating for Frank.

'We had to have him put to sleep because he was so sick, but I just couldn't do it. I had to get my brother-in-law to take him in,' he says.

It had never sat right with Frank that his old dog Snoopy remained in the grounds of his childhood home long after the family had left the property, so when Rebel died he wanted to keep his best friend close.

And he is: Rebel's ashes claim pride of place on the mantelpiece in Frank's home to this day.

Rebel's death was so gut wrenching that it was six years before Frank could even contemplate sharing his life with another dog. He left the obedience club; it felt wrong to remain involved with a sport that had been Rebel's and his 'thing'.

But then, in 2010, he started to think that perhaps it was time. His daughters were getting to an age where it would be nice for them to have a dog to romp with. Perhaps, thought Frank, he was ready to ride the rollercoaster again.

He could never have imagined just what a wild ride it would be.

If Frank was going to get another dog, he had two conditions: the new arrival had to be a Staffordshire Bull Terrier, and he had to be black and white – just like Rebel.

It took him a full year to find the right canine companion. He could have bought a black-and-white Staffy puppy many times over during that period, but the available dogs he encountered all came from large scale commercial breeding operations – better (and more notoriously) known as puppy farms. Frank wanted a healthy and robust Staffy from a reputable registered breeder, and he was prepared to wait.

When he finally met young Hellyehr Mighty Prince Billy, to use his pedigree name, at his breeder's suburban Brisbane home in early 2011, Frank knew his patience had been worthwhile.

'I wanted to make sure we got a dog that was strong, and is he ever! He looks exactly like Rebel, but he's a thoroughbred – he just wants to *go*, and he's got the strength,' Frank says. 'The breeder told me this puppy would stand over the food bowl so none of the other dogs could get in. I went from the runt of the litter to the boss of the litter.'

He named the pushy pup Billy, a shortened version of his grand kennel name, and took him home to Gladstone in April 2011, when he was nine weeks old. While his new dog was big and strong, he soon proved he was a complete pushover, especially when it came to the kids.

It frustrates Frank that Staffies still have a reputation as being dangerous or aggressive dogs. He had often experienced people hurrying away at the sight of Rebel, and resigned himself to more of the same with Billy.

'It's widespread. You take your dog for a walk and you'll always get one person who'll pick up their dog and head in the other direction. People with Staffies all across the country are used to people yelling, "Keep that dog away – I've heard about them!"' he says.

'You can get two dogs out of the same litter that are totally different. I used to run a small mobile dog washing business and I'd see it myself with the dog owners and what they'd created, some awesome dogs and some not so. The only dangerous breed is a human.'

Billy certainly grew at a rate of knots. As the breeder had hinted, he really *loved* his food.

'I had to buy one of those anti-gulp bowls with the ridges to slow him down, but he's so smart he would just flip it over,' says Frank with a laugh. 'He's a Hoover.'

But the little dog's abundant intelligence wasn't always used to outsmart his owners; Frank was also able to instill the obedience basics in Billy's eager brain.

'I started him at six months, but I was only doing the basics of puppy training,' he says. 'It has to be interesting and fun and exciting or else they won't want to do it.'

Then, in July 2012, Billy's copious cleverness and abundant appetite collided – with catastrophic consequences.

One wintry night, Frank's wife, Janet, noticed an unpleasant smell in the fridge and realised six uncooked skin-on chicken drumsticks were well and truly past their prime. She took them out and left them on the counter – making sure they were beyond the reach of a certain constantly ravenous young Staffy – and went to bed, intending to dispose of them in the outside rubbish bin first thing the next morning.

'They were still in the bag and she'd put them on the bench in the kitchen. They were safe there – the dog definitely could not get them,' Frank says. 'Unfortunately we didn't think about the cat.'

That's right. In a brazen move (and with motives that seem questionable in hindsight), Marli decided to help herself to the smelly chicken in the middle of the night.

Nobody is entirely sure what happened next, but the most likely scenario seems to be that Marli dragged the bag and its contents to the edge of the counter, where it fell onto the floor. Billy, always on the lookout for his next snack, didn't waste a moment.

'He took the bag into my daughter's bedroom, jumped up onto her bed and ate six rotten, raw chicken drumsticks. He ate the whole lot,' Frank says.

The next morning, Frank and Janet noticed the spoiled

meat was missing. 'Then I looked at Billy and he looked like a mini dairy cow. He had a big belly,' he says.

He realised immediately what had happened, but Billy seemed fine aside from his distended abdomen. Frank figured his garbage disposal of a dog had a rather upset tummy in his future, but otherwise wasn't too concerned.

The family dispersed to work and school. They didn't know that ingesting large quantities of fatty food like chicken skin can be disastrous for dogs. Why would they? Billy was infamous for eating anything he could wrap his lips around, and it hadn't caused him any problems so far.

That was about to change.

When Frank arrived home from work that afternoon, Billy was not in a good way at all. His belly was incredibly bloated, he was listless and in obvious discomfort. He just looked *sick*.

Frank raced his ailing dog straight to the vet, where the diagnosis was swift and frightening: Billy had severe acute pancreatitis.

The pancreas is a gland that secretes both insulin and enzymes that help dogs digest their food. Consuming lots of fatty food overloads the pancreas, causing it to become suddenly and severely inflamed. This is called pancreatitis. Symptoms include severe abdominal pain, vomiting and diarrhoea, dehydration and – as in Billy's case – bloating.

These digestive enzymes are usually only active in the small intestine, but when a dog has pancreatitis the enzymes damage the pancreas and surrounding tissue. If left untreated, enzymes from the pancreas can actually digest organs and tissue – the pancreas can essentially die off.

Some dog breeds are more prone to developing pancreatitis than others, including schnauzers, cocker spaniels and Yorkshire terriers.

Dogs with severe acute pancreatitis can also get peritonitis (inflammation of the tissue that lines the inner wall of the abdomen and covers most abdominal organs), sepsis (blood poisoning), and cardiovascular problems.

In Billy's case, he was also at risk of bacterial infection because the chicken was raw and spoiled.

Put simply, Billy was in big, *big* trouble.

'They took a blood sample, and I'm not joking, it looked like strawberry milk. That was how much fat was in his blood stream. It made me feel ill,' says Frank. 'If the drumsticks didn't have the skin on them it wouldn't have been a problem. He would have had an upset stomach, but nothing else. The skin has a high fat content.'

Billy was rushed into surgery, where vets repeatedly flushed his pancreas.

'That's all they can do – try to flush it out. Some of his pancreas had already died,' Frank says. 'Then they just stitched him up and told us to expect the worst. They told me he probably had a 49 per cent chance of survival.

'They said, "It's up to Billy now – if he wants to live, he'll live."'

And if by some miracle Billy did pull through, the vets warned Frank that his dog would almost certainly have diabetes for the rest of his life.

Frank couldn't believe what he was hearing. Less than twenty-four hours ago, his eighteen-month-old dog had been racing around the house, his normal, healthy, mischievous self. Now he was at death's door.

The Braes family rallied, but they were all struggling with the shocking turn of events. The worst part was the uncertainty: nobody could give Frank any assurances that Billy would make it, or whether he would have any quality of life if he lived.

'We weren't coping. My daughter at that stage was only about four, so I was trying to be strong for her. Even the vet said she was a mess, but she had to try to be strong for me,' he says. 'It was pretty heart wrenching for all of us, because we didn't know where it was going. It was a real grey area.'

Frank took Billy's predicament the hardest, because he blamed himself. He's a firm believer in personal responsibility and couldn't help but feel he had been too complacent about the safety of his loveable 'boofhead'.

'I believe I caused that. I hold myself accountable. We could have put the chicken in a container. We could have made sure it was somewhere safer,' he says. 'We can't even blame the cat, although we'd like to!'

Though he wished desperately that he could turn back the clock, all Frank could really do was wait. For a full week, Billy lay in a cage at the vet hospital, his front leg shaved to accommodate an intravenous drip that continued to pump in fluids to flush out his struggling system.

Frank, Janet and the kids visited every day. Most days

they were able to take Billy – and his drip – for a short walk outside. But he just wasn't the same dog.

'Every time I went in and saw him with this drip in him,' says Frank, 'I could see that he wanted to be happy, but he couldn't be.'

Even though he was mobile for short periods, the sad fact remained that the days were ticking by and Billy simply wasn't getting better. It seemed his pancreas was too badly damaged. He continued to walk a tightrope between life and death, and one wobble in the wrong direction would be all it took.

'Sometimes they don't get better; they get worse. There was no change and the vet said we were almost at that point where we were just going to have to let him go,' Frank says.

That possibility was unbearable. As well as being food obsessed, Billy was a ball fanatic, and so in a last ditch effort to spark his warrior spirit Frank employed a secret weapon.

'I took his old blue tennis ball and stuck it in his cage,' he says. 'He looked like he perked up a bit, even though he could hardly move.'

Sure enough, the next day the vet rang Frank to say that Billy's condition had slightly improved. Once again, Frank was stunned. Miraculously, the soggy old ball had done the trick!

The vet felt that Billy's condition was more likely to continue improving if he was in a familiar environment, so after emergency treatment costing close to $2000 he was allowed to go home on the condition that he follow a strict low-fat diet.

'They said, "If he wants to eat, give him skinless chicken breast with rice and veggies." How ironic! I cringed,' Frank says.

Day by day, brave Billy grew stronger. If Frank thought the ordeal might have taught his dog a lesson about moderation, he was mistaken.

'He's just ploughed ahead. He never stopped his eating habits, though he's not allowed to eat anything fatty,' he says. 'He has his own biscuits [dry food] and he gets that every night, and toast crusts in the morning. He does get a few treats every now and then, but it's rare.'

It took about six months for Billy to recover fully, but finally he was his old self again. Frank often wonders what it was that revived Billy just when all seemed lost. He never did develop diabetes either. His comeback was truly against the odds.

'He wasn't supposed to live, but I think it was something about his fighting spirit – he didn't want to go,' he says. 'We do tend to take them for granted a bit until something like this happens.'

The tennis ball certainly helped, too. Frank put it in a Ziploc bag and sealed it tight. It remains on the mantelpiece, unopened to this day, a constant reminder that even on the darkest nights, there is hope.

Once Billy was fighting fit again, Frank made a decision. The days of sporadic puppy training were over. He couldn't undo the past, but Billy had been given a second chance and Frank wanted to help him make the most of it. Maybe he could even dispel some myths and break down some of the stigma around Staffies as a breed while he was at it.

'All we can do is move forward and that's what we're doing now,' he says. 'What happened to Billy was one of the reasons I said, "I'm going to make this dog special."'

With Billy back on his paws, Frank wasn't about to let the grass grow under them. He started training at a local park and signed himself and Billy up for a forthcoming trial in Rockhampton, 100 kilometres away.

Then they began training in earnest. 'I started training him by myself, and we trained six nights a week – rain, hail or shine. Billy just loved doing it,' Frank says.

To earn his Community Companion Dog title, Billy needed three scores of 85 or higher out of 100. He scored 93 in the Rockhampton trial, and followed that impressive effort with 96 and 97 in subsequent trials back at Gladstone. He had won the title!

Frank wasn't surprised that Billy breezed through those first few competitions. 'The first couple of levels of obedience trialling are, to me, fairly basic, so he had no trouble at all with those,' he says.

Next the pair travelled back to Rockhampton to compete for a title at the next level, Companion Dog, where Billy demonstrated that even obedience trialling prodigies can have off days.

'Unfortunately it was freezing and raining, and he did not work well in those conditions,' says Frank.

Back home, he doubled down on Billy's training, working hard to get his clever dog comfortable with as many different situations and conditions as possible.

'I train next to a runway because you want your dog to face as many distractions as you can and not lose concentration,' he says. 'If there's a jet plane landing next to you and you tell your dog to drop and he drops, you know he's got it down.'

In June 2015, Frank and Billy travelled to the outer suburbs of Brisbane to compete in both the state and national Companion Dog titles. Once again, Billy didn't quite make the cut in the state titles.

'In the Queensland titles Billy noticed I was nervous and he did almost everything he was not supposed to do,' says Frank. 'He lost concentration because he was sniffing the scent of sausages in the air.'

Billy's momentary lapse meant he missed Frank's hand signal for 'stay' and mistakenly followed his master. He was disqualified, but still impressed the judges. 'There was one judge there and everyone was *oohing* and *aahing* and I found out later that he gave us 30 out of 30, and he doesn't give anybody high scores,' Frank says.

Billy redeemed himself the next day at the national titles. He not only qualified as a Companion Dog, he took first place from a field of nineteen dogs with a score of 190/200.

He earned his state Companion Dog title in 2016, after scoring 192/200 and 195/200 in his second and third attempts.

'We're either disqualified or we're first – there is no in between with Billy!'

Billy is eight now and has competed in six obedience trials. Where his predecessor, Rebel, turned heads with a career average of 190 out of 200, Billy has performed even better: his average stands at 192 out of 200.

For Frank, there are few things sweeter than sharing a moment of victory with his best mate – especially when he came so close to losing Billy altogether.

'I haven't achieved anything better. There isn't a nicer feeling than when you win something, but when it's with an animal that can't speak English it's a real achievement,' he says. 'The bond is what it's all about.'

He would love to see how much further Billy can take his obedience career, but busy family life doesn't leave as much time for obedience training these days. Not that Frank intends to put his feet up – far from it. He's planning to give dog agility a go next.

'I think Billy would be well suited to it. Even though he's a bit older now, he's such an athletic dog. He can just run,' he says. 'It's a challenge for me, plus it will be fun for him.'

And Billy is all about having fun; he seems to want to wring as much adventure from this crazy rollercoaster ride as he can. There have been soaring highs and crashing lows for both Billy and Frank, but through it all they've been together – and that is truly what matters.

Back from the brink of death with an owner whose mission in life is to make sure he has fun – is it any wonder Billy sees life as a miracle?

MORE INFORMATION

MAGGIE

Instagram: @maggiethewunderdog

FERGUS

Facebook: fergusgoldenretrieversurvivor

KALU

Instagram: @kaluthewonderdog
Facebook: Animal-SOS-Sri-Lanka
www.animalsos-sl.com

GUY

Facebook: ADogsDreamRescueOakvilleON

CHLOE

Instagram: @bikerdogchloe
Facebook: iridewithchloe

JAKE

Instagram: @jakethefirepibble
Facebook: JaketheFirePibble

PEDRO

Instagram: @bawabali_official
Facebook: bawabali
www.bawabali.com

MILLIE

Facebook: greyhoundrescueNSW & norasfosterhounds
www.greyhoundrescue.com.au

DARE

Facebook: DaredevilTheHusky

ROO

Instagram: @livelikeroofoundation
Facebook: livelikeroo
livelikeroo.org

JAX

Facebook: southaustraliapolice
gsdrescuesa.com.au

MOLLY

Instagram: @rottenpaws

ACKNOWLEDGEMENTS

My sincerest and most gushing thanks go to the amazing owners of all the incredible dogs featured in this book. Most of the time, writing books about inspirational dogs means I have to ask people to relive some of their worst experiences, to share with me their fear and vulnerability, to talk about loss and heartache. It is truly an honour and a privilege that you have trusted me to tell your dogs' stories, and in a way, your own. Thank you from the bottom of my heart.

I also have a ton of gratitude for my editors at Penguin Random House, especially Johannes Jakob, Cate Blake and Alison Urquhart. I seriously can't believe you guys keep letting me do this dream job. Please never stop.

A massive thanks to Brendan Carmel, veterinarian and co-host of the brilliant *VetGurus* podcast, for cheerfully and swiftly responding to all my '*What does this mean?*' emails. There is a *lot* of medical jargon in this book, and it's largely thanks to Brendan that it's all correct.

Thanks to everyone who buys, borrows and reads my books. It goes without saying that I would not be doing this without you. Extra thanks to those of you who have reached out to tell me you've loved reading about these astonishing dogs, and apologies to those I've made cry.

I've got to thank my mad menagerie: Tex, Delilah and Coco the dogs; Raphaella and Cookie the guinea pigs; and Elsa the goldfish. Yes, I am aware you cannot read, but you have been an invaluable source of joy and support nonetheless.

So much love to my family and friends, who buy my books and read my books and badger other people to do the same. Special shoutout to my best friend in the cosmos, Karlie. I am so lucky to know you. We should all be fortunate enough to have a BFF who'll fly to another state just to run the raffle at a book event.

Thanks to wine and chocolate, two of my most enduring loves.

And, as ever, love and gratitude that no words can properly express to my husband, Mark, and our kiddo. None of this exists without you.

INCREDIBLE
DOG
JOURNEYS

*AMAZING
TRUE STORIES OF
EXCEPTIONAL
DOGS*

LAURA GREAVES

INSPIRATIONAL TALES OF THE WORLD'S
HARDEST WORKING DOGS

DOGS
with

JOBS

LAURA GREAVES

The RESCUERS

INCREDIBLE STORIES OF LIFE-SAVING DOGS

LAURA GREAVES

Discover a
new favourite

Visit **penguin.com.au/readmore**